IDEAS from the

ARITHMETIC TEACHER
Grades 1–4   Primary

IDEAS from the

ARITHMETIC TEACHER

Grades 1–4   Primary

compiled by

George Immerzeel

Melvin Thomas

from original IDEAS prepared by

George Bright

Marilyn Burns

Joan Duea

George Immerzeel

Earl Ockenga

Don Wiederanders

Donald W. Scheuer, Jr.

David E. Williams

M. Bernadine Tabler

Marilyn Hall Jacobson

Copyright © 1982 by

The National Council of Teachers of Mathematics, Inc.
1906 Association Drive, Reston, Virginia 22091

Printed in the United States of America

ISBN 0-87353-189-2

Second printing 1985
Third printing 1987
Fourth printing 1988
Fifth printing 1990

Introduction

The IDEAS section has been a feature of the *Arithmetic Teacher* since 1971. This collection has been selected from those activities appropriate for students in grades 1 through 4. The selections have been reprinted just as they originally appeared in the journal.

On one side of each page you will find the Pupil Activity Sheet; the teacher directions are on the reverse. This booklet has been perforated so that the pages can be easily removed and reproduced for classroom use. We suggest that you make a file of these pages or punch them for storage in a loose-leaf binder. Copies should be kept in the same file or binder so that you can use them when they are needed.

This volume has been topically arranged so that IDEAS for computational skills, for example, appear in one section, IDEAS for problem solving are grouped in another section, and so on. Suggested grade levels appear in the teacher directions for each IDEAS sheet.

Table of Contents

IDEAS for Numeration .... Page 1

IDEAS for Computation .... Page 13

IDEAS for Geometry .... Page 53

IDEAS for Measurement .... Page 77

IDEAS for Problem Solving .... Page 95

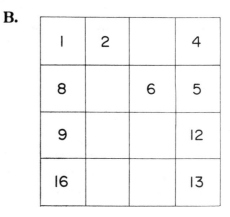

Name _____

Fill in the blanks in each table.

A.

1		3	4
5	6		8
9	10		12
13			16

B.

1	2		4
8		6	5
9			12
16			13

C.

1		9	
2	7	10	15
4	5	12	13

D.

13		15	
12	11		9
5	6		
	3	2	1

E.

		14	13
9			12
	7		5
	2	3	

F.

	9		1
15		7	
	11		3
13		5	4

 For Teachers

Objective: Experience with numeration patterns

Grade level: 1 or 2

Directions for teachers:

Remove the student worksheet and reproduce a copy for each student. The temptation to use this lesson primarily as a "follow the directions" lesson should be avoided. The less directive the teacher can be, the more the student will be challenged to see the pattern in the table.

Directions for students:

Each table is to have the numbers 1 to 16 in it. Some numbers are missing. See if you can decide what number to put in each blank space.

Comments: You may have to ask leading questions to get the first graders started on each table. A subtle emphasis on correct numeral formation might well be included if it doesn't detract from the focus on patterns.

Variations on this experience might include using a 3-by-3 table for beginners or starting the counting sequence with some number other than 1 for more advanced students.

Name _____

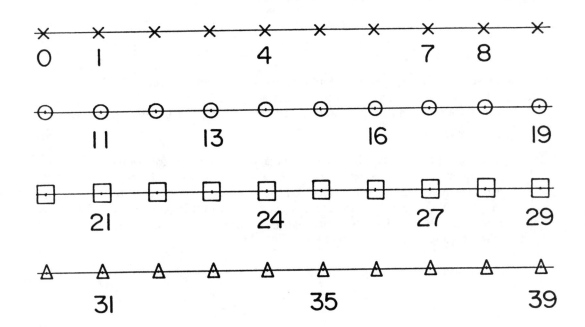

How are the points for these numbers marked?

2 _____	13 _____	7 _____
22 _____	33 _____	12 _____
6 _____	30 _____	39 _____
20 _____	21 _____	26 _____
32 _____	38 _____	35 _____
5 _____	15 _____	25 _____
9 _____	28 _____	34 _____

 **For Teachers**

Objective: Experience with basic numeration patterns

Levels: 1 or 2

Directions for teachers:

1. Remove the activity sheet and reproduce a copy for each student.
2. Read the instructions and have the students go to work.
3. Observe your students as they work to be certain that they understand what they are to do.

Comments: The patterns within our numeration system are frequently built entirely on counting experiences and numeral-writing projects. This type of experience forces the student to focus on the numerals as they relate to to each other. You can readily expand this experience to other portions of the number line. By varying the points that are named, you can make the activity sheets easier or more challenging.

Clues to answers: There are 5 ✕'s, 3 ◯'s, 6 ▢'s, and 7 △'s.

I D E A S

Team _____

_____

How many?

_____

_____

* * * * * * *

Team guess _____

Team count _____   Team score _____

Objective: Experience in estimating and counting.   Levels: 1 or 2

Directions for teachers:

1. Remove the activity sheet and reproduce a copy for each team.
2. Form teams of four students each.
3. Have each team record their *collective guess*.
4. Have each *team* arrive at a *count*.
5. Use this table to score each team.

Guess	80 to 90	75 to 95	70 to 100
Points	5	3	1
Count	85	84 to 86	83 or 87

6. Discuss the procedures used in estimating and counting by the various teams.

Comments: A team of four has definite advantages. Four students will generally provide leadership and sufficient content input to insure group progress. Learning to work effectively as a member of a small group is a major educational objective and can help to meet our needs to individualize instruction.

Other similar task sheets which challenge the best team or are appropriate for the slowest team in your class, can be designed.

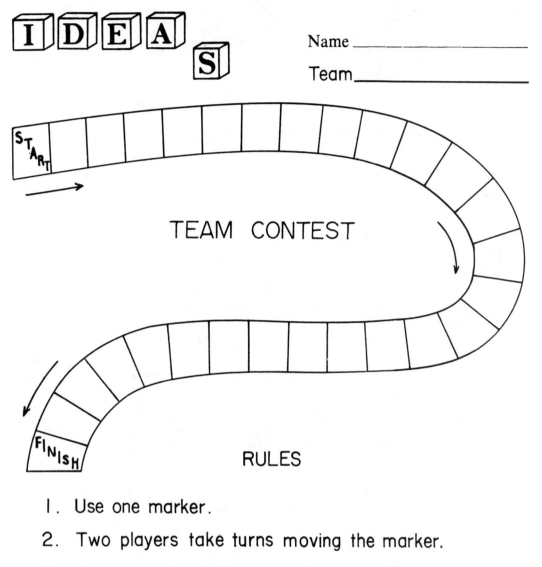

IDEAS

Name _____

Team _____

TEAM CONTEST

RULES

1. Use one marker.
2. Two players take turns moving the marker.
3. On each turn, the player may move the marker 1, 2, 3, 4, or 5 spaces.
4. The player who moves onto the FINISH is the winner.
5. The loser must put his initials <u>on the winner's</u> game sheet.
6. The <u>team</u> with the largest number of initials is the winner.

Initials of losers:

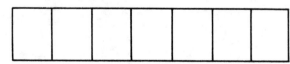

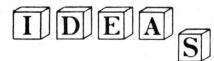

Objective: Experience with addition in a strategy-oriented game.

Levels: 2 or 3

Directions for teachers:

1. Remove the activity sheet and reproduce a copy for each student.
2. Form teams of four students each.
3. Use a marker to play the game. Have teams practice the game to develop playing skill and a strategy for winning.
4. Have each team member play the game with members of other teams, but a team member should play no more than two games with the same opponent.
5. After each game the loser must put his initials in one of the rectangles on the bottom of the winners paper.
6. The team whose members have the largest number of initials is the winner.

Comments: The need to either plan ahead or learn from experience is obvious in this game. Once both players have perfected the winning strategy, the person who starts can always win—thus making it "no game." Variations of the game can be made by changing the number of permissible moves or the length of the "track."

EVEN SPLITS

Take some counters

Will they split
into 2 groups
the same size?

If YES, color in the space
with that number

If NO, put an X on that
number

DO THIS FOR ALL THE NUMBERS BELOW

1	2	3	4	5	6	7	8	9	10
11	12	13	14	15	16	17	18	19	20
21	22	23	24	25	26	27	28	29	30

What's the pattern? _____

 For Teachers

Level: 1, 2, 3

Objective: To develop the concept of even and odd numbers

Directions for teachers:

1. Duplicate a worksheet for each child.
2. Make sure they understand the directions.

3. When the children have completed their work, introduce the terms *even* for the numbers colored and *odd* for those with an X.

Going further:

1. What would happen to zero?
2. Do the activity again, but splitting into 3 piles instead. Investigate the patterns.

Name_____

Pick any number from 1 to 9 and write it in the box

START

Now, in your head, add 9 to the number in the box, and write the sum here. (Don't write the 9)

Continue adding 9 until you get to the double line

ANSWER THESE QUESTIONS:

1)   What's the pattern of the numbers in the 1s place? _____

_____

2)   What's the pattern of the numbers in the 10s and 100s places?_____

_____

3)   Add the digits of each number you wrote. What's the pattern?_____

_____

(If you add the digits and you get a 2-digit answer, add once more;
for example, 39. 3 + 9 = 12. 1 + 2 = 3.

 For Teachers

Level: 2, 3, 4, 5

Objective: To provide addition drill; to investigate number patterns

Directions for teachers:

1. Duplicate a worksheet for each child.
2. Make sure they understand the directions.

3. Have the children compare their results with others.

Going further:

1. Try the activity again adding 8s instead of 9s. Investigate the patterns.
2. Investigate what happens when adding other numbers also.

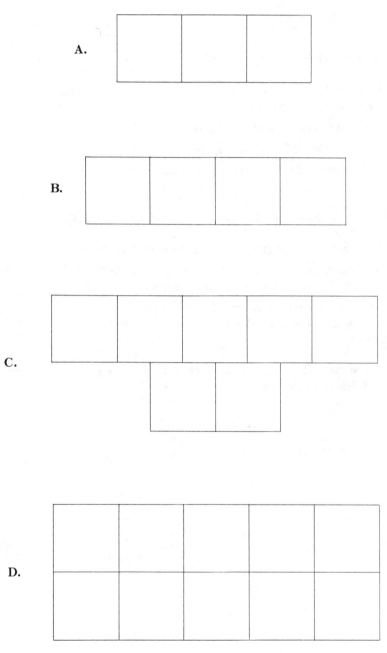

Directions: To put one bean in the first square, two beans in the
second square, three beans in the third square, how
many beans will it take for each set of squares?

A.

B.

C.

D.

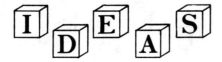 For Teachers

Objective: Experience in addition that relates to simple
number patterns.

Grade level: 1, 2, or 3

Directions for teachers:

1. Tear out the page and either reproduce the page in classroom numbers
    or place it in the mathematics corner.
2. For each worksheet provide a handful of lima beans.
3. Introduce the activity during a few minutes in mathematics class.
4. Discuss the students' answers and how they arrived at them.

Comments: You can change the rules and develop many other experiences.

1. Put 1 bean in the first square, 3 in the next, 5 in the next, and so on.
2. How many beans would you need to put 10 in the first, 20 in the second, and 30 in the third until all the squares are counted?
3. Put 1 bean in the first square, 2 in the second, 4 in the third, doubling the number of beans in the next square until there are beans in each square.

    If you encourage them the students will often suggest rules of their own that other students can try.

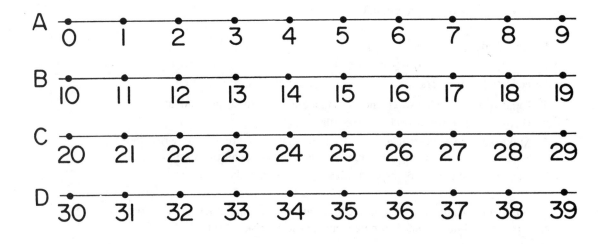

Which number line has a point for these numbers?

_____ 3 + 5	_____ 20 + 7	_____ 12 + 13
_____ 15 + 10	_____ 17 + 8	_____ 10 + 10
_____ 23 + 11	_____ 12 + 0	_____ 16 + 3
_____ 19 + 11	_____ 26 + 4	_____ 12 + 15
_____ 3 + 7	_____ 5 + 4	_____ 15 + 14
_____ 23 + 12	_____ 17 + 18	_____ 20 + 12

For Teachers

Objective: Experience in estimating the sum

Levels: 2 or 3

Directions for teachers:

1. Remove the activity sheet and reproduce a copy for each student.
2. Have students study each number line.
3. Make sure that the students understand that they are not to write the sum but only to identify the number line that contains the sum.
4. Encourage students to respond without computing the sum.

Comments: Anticipate that many students will compute the sum before they respond. Students need to be encouraged to be risk takers.

Clues to answers: 2 A's, 3 B's, 7 C's, 6 D's.

Name _____

Find the winner!

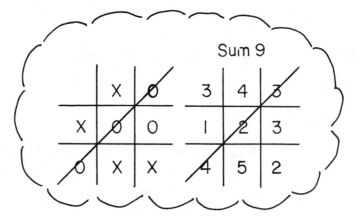

Sum 9

X	O	3	4	3
X	O	O	1	2	3
O	X	X	4	5	2

Sum 10

2	5	1
1	4	5
6	2	3

Sum 8

3	4	2
5	3	1
4	2	2

Sum 7

2	3	3
5	2	1
4	1	2

Sum 9

6	3	5
2	0	1
4	2	4

Sum 6

2	4	1
1	2	4
3	1	3

Sum 10

5	2	6
4	5	3
2	4	1

Objective: Experience in recognizing three addends with a specific sum

Levels: 1 or 2

Directions for teachers:

1. Remove the activity sheet and reproduce a copy for each student.

2. Discuss the example. Be sure students realize that two criteria must be met,
   (*a*) three numbers in a row (like tic-tac-toe), and
   (*b*) "add up to" the indicated sum.

3. Have students check their "winners" with a friend.

Comments: You may wish to make up other "game boards" to meet the individual needs of your students. Avoid having more than one "winner."

Name _____

Mark each play to
find the winner.

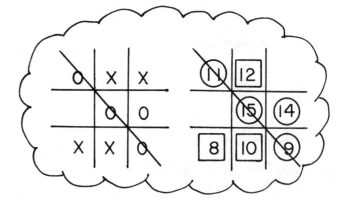

8	12	13
7	11	9
6	10	14

Plays

□ = 6 + 5   □ = 2 + 4

○ = 8 + 6   ○ = 7 + 6

□ = 5 + 3   □ = 4 + 3

○ = 8 + 2   ○ = 7 + 5

16	3	12
11	9	4
7	13	8

Plays

□ = 9 + 7   □ = 10 − 6

○ = 11 − 3   ○ = 7 + 6

□ = 12 − 9   □ = 6 + 5

○ = 7 + 5   ○ = 15 − 8

11	8	9
4	6	5
15	17	14

Plays

3 + ○ = 12   7 + ○ = 15

14 − 8 = □   □ = 3 + 8

6 + 9 = ○   9 + ○ = 14

□ + 4 = 11   6 + 8 = □

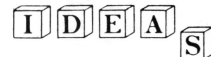 For Teachers

Objective: Experience with the basic facts of addition and subtraction

Levels: 3 or 4

Directions for teachers:

1. Remove the activity sheet and reproduce a copy for each student.
2. Study the example. Note that one player marks with ☐ and the other with ○.
3. Make sure the directions are understood. (That is, the first player puts a ☐ around 11, the second player puts a ○ around 14, and so on. Three like marks in a row is a winner.)

Comments: Note that the game is a take-off on the familiar tic-tac-toe. A similar experience with multiplication facts and missing factor equations (3 × ☐ = 21, and so on) may be appropriate for your students. Supplemental exercises are easily created if you "play the game" as you list the equations. The fact that it is difficult to "win" doesn't seem to affect the students' enthusiasm for playing the game.

 Name _____

Find the sum of the numbers in each table.

A.

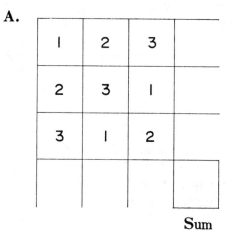

1	2	3	
2	3	1	
3	1	2	

Sum

B.

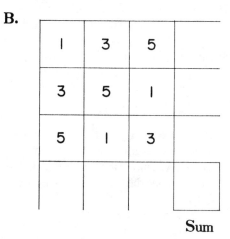

1	3	5	
3	5	1	
5	1	3	

Sum

C.

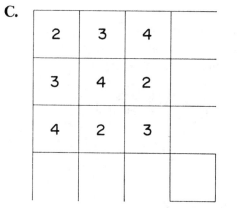

2	3	4	
3	4	2	
4	2	3	

Sum

D.

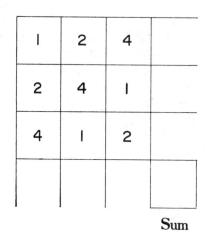

1	2	4	
2	4	1	
4	1	2	

Sum

E.

4	5	6	
5	6	4	
6	4	5	

Sum

F.

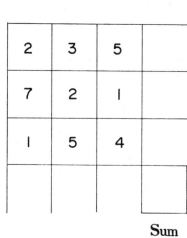

2	3	5	
7	2	1	
1	5	4	

Sum

 For Teachers

Objective: Experience with computation patterns involving the associative and commutative properties for addition

Grade level: 2 or 3

Directions for teachers:

Reproduce a copy of the worksheet for each student. You will want to be as nondirective as possible. Encourage independence on the part of each student. When most of the students have finished, discuss each table. Draw out as many different student techniques for finding the sum as possible. The heart of this experience is in the sharing of insights by students. Since there is no incorrect technique, you can leave value judgments up to the individual student.

Comments: Insights are a very personal thing. Even those shared by peers are not always communicated. Since the teacher's role is that of drawing out student insights, the temptation to introduce the formal language of the mathematics involved is diminished.

You may wish to expand on this experience by having students construct similar tables for each other, or you may wish to construct others that focus on larger numbers.

Answers

A. 18   B. 27   C. 27   D. 21   E. 45   F. 30

IDEAS

Name _____

Put the letters on the right box.

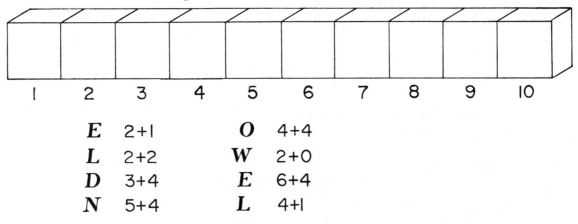

1	2	3	4	5	6	7	8	9	10

E	2+1	*O*	4+4
L	2+2	*W*	2+0
D	3+4	*E*	6+4
N	5+4	*L*	4+1

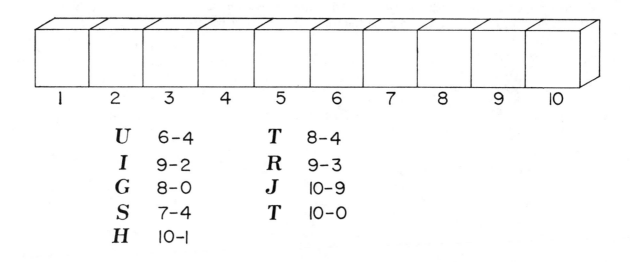

1	2	3	4	5	6	7	8	9	10

U	6-4	*T*	8-4
I	9-2	*R*	9-3
G	8-0	*J*	10-9
S	7-4	*T*	10-0
H	10-1		

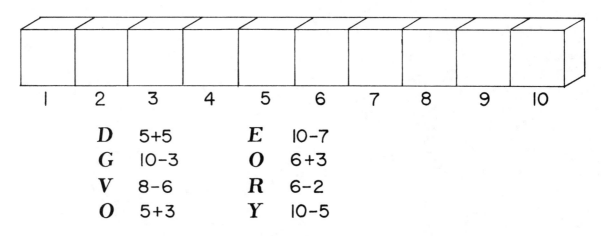

1	2	3	4	5	6	7	8	9	10

D	5+5	*E*	10-7
G	10-3	*O*	6+3
V	8-6	*R*	6-2
O	5+3	*Y*	10-5

Objective: Experience with ordering numbers identified by their basic fact names

Levels: 1 or 2

Directions for teachers:

1. Give each student a copy of the activity sheet.
2. Read the directions aloud then ask: "Which box should we put the letter *E* on?"
3. Have the students go ahead.
4. Observe each student as he works. Help him read the message as he finishes lettering each row of boxes.

Comments: Students with varying abilities and backgrounds of experience should be expected to attack this activity differently. Those who cannot read the message confidently can be given feedback after a brief glance from the teacher.

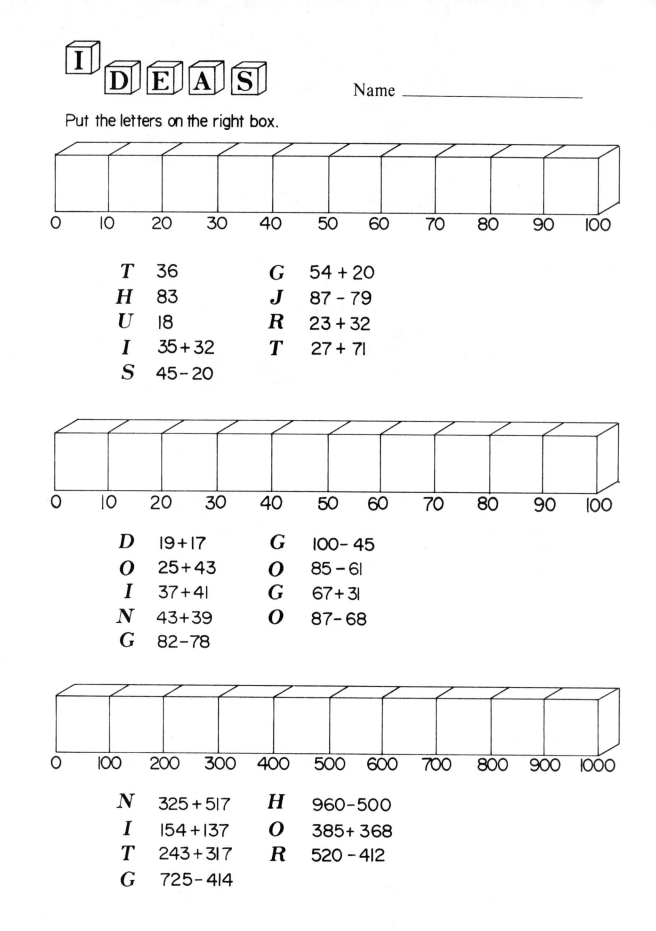

IDEAS

Name _____

Put the letters on the right box.

	0	10	20	30	40	50	60	70	80	90	100

T	36		*G*	54 + 20
H	83		*J*	87 − 79
U	18		*R*	23 + 32
I	35 + 32		*T*	27 + 71
S	45 − 20			

	0	10	20	30	40	50	60	70	80	90	100

D	19 + 17		*G*	100 − 45
O	25 + 43		*O*	85 − 61
I	37 + 41		*G*	67 + 31
N	43 + 39		*O*	87 − 68
G	82 − 78			

	0	100	200	300	400	500	600	700	800	900	1000

N	325 + 517		*H*	960 − 500
I	154 + 137		*O*	385 + 368
T	243 + 317		*R*	520 − 412
G	725 − 414			

Objective: Experience in ordering numbers that encourages estimation rather than computation

Levels: 2 or 3

Directions for teachers:

1. Give each student a copy of the activity sheet.
2. Read the directions aloud. Then ask: "Which of the first three numbers would go in the second box?" (18) "What letter should you put on the second box?" (U) "Which letter goes on the box between 80 and 90?" (H)
3. Have the students proceed with the activity.
4. After they have worked for a few minutes, comment: "If you put each letter on the correct box you will be able to read the message."

Comments: After they have worked for a few minutes, you may also wish to encourage them to estimate by commenting, "Some of you seem to be able to figure out which box to put each letter on without computing." Anticipate that some students will try to unscramble the letters rather than estimate each number. We hope this will prove to be an inefficient approach.

Directions: Cut out the squares. Fit them together so that the
edges that touch name the same number.

4	9	I	
4 ... 10	1+4 ... 8	3+4	6
2	6		2+5
3+5	0+2	6+1	
9+1 ... 2+2	2+6 ... 9	6+2	3
4+5	4+4		4+2
	6	7	8
5 ... 2+1	6+4	7+2	9 ... 8
1+3	3+4	7	
5+1	3+2	7	
7 ... 6+3	5	10	3+3 ... 3+2
	0+1	5	8

🄸🄳🄴🄰🅂
for Levels 1 or 2

Objective: Experience with the concept of equals.

Directions:
1. Provide each student with a copy of the appropriate activity sheet and a pair of scissors.
2. If necessary, give the hint that when the squares are fit together correctly, a 4 by 4 square is once again found.

Comments: The fewer directions required the better. Students need experience in figuring things out for themselves. As the student progresses with each puzzle, his decisions receive immediate reinforcement.

Key

```
     6    5    3
  7 + 8 + 4 + 6
    10    4   10
  5 + 9 + 2 + 7
     5    8    9
  1 + 6 + 8 + 7
     7    9    8
```

 Name _____

Directions: Cut out the 16 squares. Fit them together so that the edges that touch name the same number.

10-5 6 9-1 8-1	8 10-7 15-5 12-2	9-4 5 	 11-2 2
6 6-2 12-6 10-2	7 10 6-4 9-6	4-0 7 	 0 12-3
7-4 2 4	3 10-6 9-2 	10 8-3 4 	4 3 5
9 8 3	 1 8-8 5	 9 7-6 9-3	8-6 4 7-3

for Levels 2 or 3

Objective: Experience with the concept of equals.

Directions:
1. Provide each student with a copy of the appropriate activity sheet and a pair of scissors.
2. If necessary, give the hint that when the squares are fit together correctly, a 4 by 4 square is once again found.

Comments: The fewer directions required the better. Students need experience in figuring things out for themselves. As the student progresses with each puzzle, his decisions receive immediate reinforcement.

Key

```
    9    I    0
 -2 +6 +5 +9-
    4    6    8
 -4 +8 +7 +3-
    3   10    2
 -5 +10+ 3 +4-
    5    4    7
```

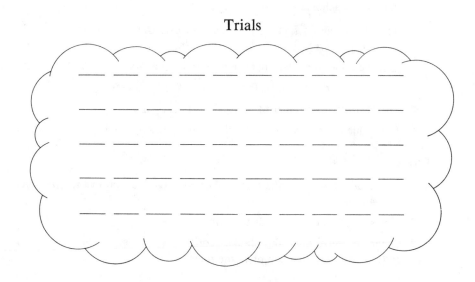

Name _____

Name _____

1. Roll your cubes and write the sums in the blanks.

Trials

————— ————— ————— ————— —————

————— ————— ————— ————— —————

————— ————— ————— ————— —————

————— ————— ————— ————— —————

————— ————— ————— ————— —————

2. Make one mark (/) for each time you got each sum.

Sum									
Tally									
Totals									

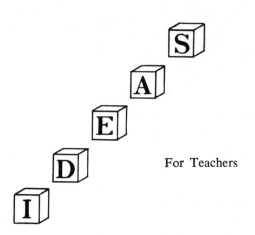

For Teachers

Objective: Experience recording data.

Grade level: 1, 2, or 3

Directions for teachers:

1. Take three one-inch cubes for each pair of students (use only two cubes for first graders).

2. On one cube use a felt marker to number the sides 1, 2, 3, 4, 5, and 6.

3. On a second cube number the sides 4, 4, 5, 5, 6, and 6.

4. On a third cube number the sides 0, 0, 1, 1, 2, and 2.

5. Reproduce one copy of the student worksheet for each pair of students.

Directions for students:

1. One student is to roll the three cubes and give the sum of the three faces that are up.

2. The second student records the sum in the blanks.

3. After you have filled the blanks (completed 50 rolls), you are to make tally marks and then complete the table.

Comments: After most of the students have rolled their cubes, stop the class and discuss the largest sum, smallest sum, and the number of different sums. Complete the sums row for the table. Also explain how to make tally marks in the boxes in the table.

The possible sums for the cubes described are 5, 6, 7, $\cdots$, and 14. Our choice of numbers for the sides of the cubes makes 9 and 10 the most likely sums. If you wish to place greater emphasis on lower sums, lower the numbers on the second cube. If greater emphasis on larger sums is desired, increase the numbers on the third cube.

With first graders, only two of the cubes might be used the first time, but the same worksheet could be used.

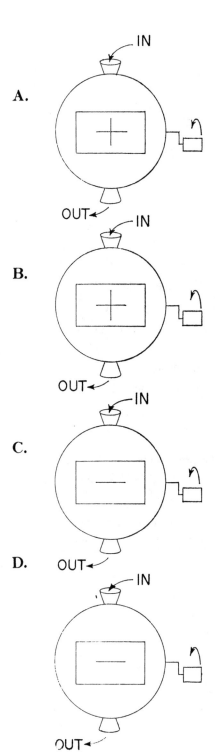

Study the table. Complete the entries.

A.

IN	2	3	4	5	7	10
OUT	5	6				

B.

IN	0	5	6	2	10	8
OUT	5	10				

C.

IN	7	3	4	6	5	9
OUT	5	1				

D.

IN	9	7	5	8	10	4
OUT	5	3				

IDEAS for Computation 33

Objective: Experience with addition and subtraction patterns at the basic-fact level

Grade level: 2 or 3

Directions for teachers:

1. Remove the activity sheet and reproduce a copy for each student.
2. Have the students study number machine *A* and the table beside it.
3. Complete this table working collectively, then decide what machine *A* does. *Answer:* adds 3.
4. Have students complete the table for machine *B* independently.
5. Handle the tables for machines *C* and *D* in a similar manner.

Comments: The student expects the machine to be predictable. The given entries provide the required clues to what the machine is programmed to do. Number machines are included in several basic texts. They provide a motif for the very important study of number patterns.

You may wish to extend these tables to include more difficult entries if the needs of your class warrant it. Many students like to make up machines for the rest of the class.

Answers

Machine *B:* adds 5; Machine *C:* subtracts 2; Machine *D:* subtracts 4.

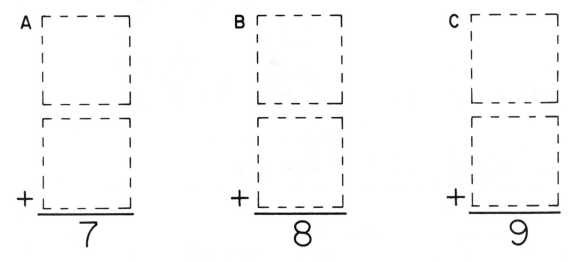

Match the number tags to the spaces.

A
```
   □
 + □
 ─────
   7
```

B
```
   □
 + □
 ─────
   8
```

C
```
   □
 + □
 ─────
   9
```

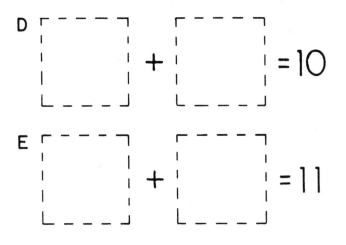

D □ + □ = 10

E □ + □ = 11

Cut out the tags.

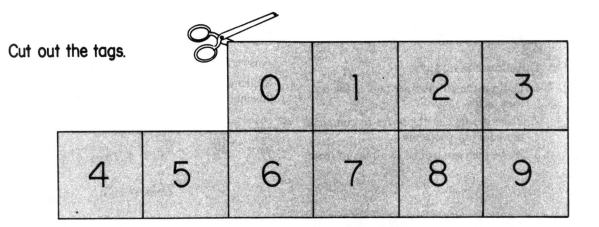

0	1	2	3
4	5	6	7	8	9

Objective: Experience with addition facts

Levels: 1, 2

Directions for teachers:

1. Remove the student activity sheet and reproduce one copy for each child.
2. Read the directions for students given below.
3. Encourage students to try various arrangements of their number tags so each tag is used once and all five examples are correct.

Directions for students:

1. Cut out the ten number tags at the bottom of the page.
2. Place the tags in the boxes to complete the addition problems.
3. Move the tags around so all ten of them are used once and every example is correct.

Comments:

After students have tried the activity alone, modifications could be introduced:

Students who have not completed all five addition examples could work together in pairs.

Students who have been successful might select any four tags and see how many of the examples can be completed. In this activity the four tags can be used more than once.

Answers:

Students have found eight solutions. The following is one:

$$
\begin{array}{llll}
A\ \boxed{4} & B\ \boxed{8} & C\ \boxed{7} & D\ \boxed{9}+\boxed{1}=10 \\
\ +\boxed{3} & \ +\boxed{0} & \ +\boxed{2} & \\
\ \overline{7} & \ \overline{8} & \ \overline{9} & E\ \boxed{5}+\boxed{6}=11
\end{array}
$$

Name_____

Match the number tags to the spaces. Use each tag only once.

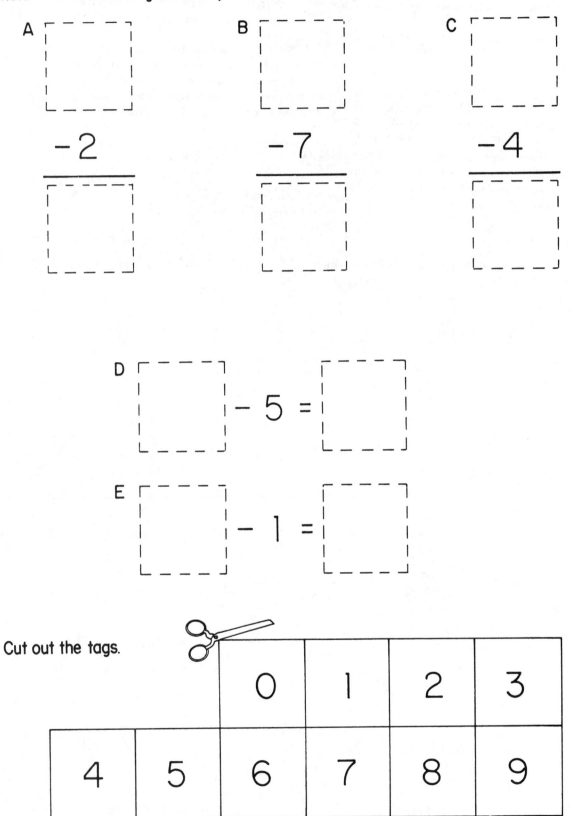

A

-2

B

-7

C

-4

D $- 5 =$

E $- 1 =$

Cut out the tags.

0	1	2	3

4	5	6	7	8	9

Objective: Experience with subtraction facts

Levels: 2, 3, 4

Directions for teachers:

1. Remove the student activity sheet and reproduce one copy for each child.
2. Encourage students to try various arrangements of their number tags so each tag is used once and all five examples are correct.

Comments:

After the students have tried the activity alone, modifications could be introduced:

The students who have not completed all five subtraction examples could work together in pairs.

Students who have been successful might be challenged to complete the examples with only five tags. In this activity, the tags could be used more than once. A scoring system could also be introduced—one point is awarded for every correctly completed example.

Answers:

Students have found six solutions. The following is one.

$$A \quad \frac{\boxed{8}}{\boxed{6}} \frac{-2}{} \qquad B \quad \frac{\boxed{7}}{\boxed{0}} \frac{-7}{} \qquad C \quad \frac{\boxed{5}}{\boxed{1}} \frac{-4}{} \qquad D \quad \boxed{9} - 5 = \boxed{4}$$

$$E \quad \boxed{3} - 1 = \boxed{2}$$

NAMING NUMBERS

RULES:

- Take turns.
- Pick two numbers.
- Mark one picture that tells about your numbers.
- Three pictures in a line wins.

1 2 3
1 2 3

GAME BOARD

Naming Numbers

Objective: Experiences with matching sets of objects to selected numbers

Levels: K–1

Directions for teachers:

1. Remove the student activity sheet. Make a transparency and at least one copy for each pair of students.
2. Using the transparency, play the game (teacher vs. students) so the students learn the rules.

Directions for pairs of students:

1. Take turns pointing to two numbers.
2. Find one picture that tells about your numbers and mark it. (For example, a child that points to "2" and "3," could mark a picture with 5 objects. Children can use *X*s and *O*s or crayons of different colors.)
3. The winner is the first player to get three pictures marked in a row.

IDEAS

SPOTTING SUMS

RULES: Take turns.

1. Place the arrows on two of the numbers at the right.
2. Add these numbers.
3. Mark the answer on the game board with your mark, X or O.

The winner is the first one to get three marks in a line.

1 2 3
4 5 6
7 8 9

GAME BOARD

10	5	8	3
2	12	16	15
14	17	11	6
7	4	13	9

Spotting Sums

Objective: Experiences with addition,
focusing on addends
needed to get a desired sum

Levels: 2, 3

Directions for teachers:

1. Remove the student activity sheet
   and make a transparency and at
   least one copy for each pair of students.

2. Using the transparency, play the
   game (teacher vs. students) so the
   students learn the rules.

Directions for pairs of students:

1. Cut out the arrows at the bottom of
   the page.

2. Sign your name by *X* or *O* at the top
   of the page.

3. Read the rules before playing the
   game.

PLAY ESTIMATING ADDITION

Circle two numbers.

33	36	45	26	9	53	3	12	43
	19	16	23	49	29	32	42	

Add the numbers you circled.

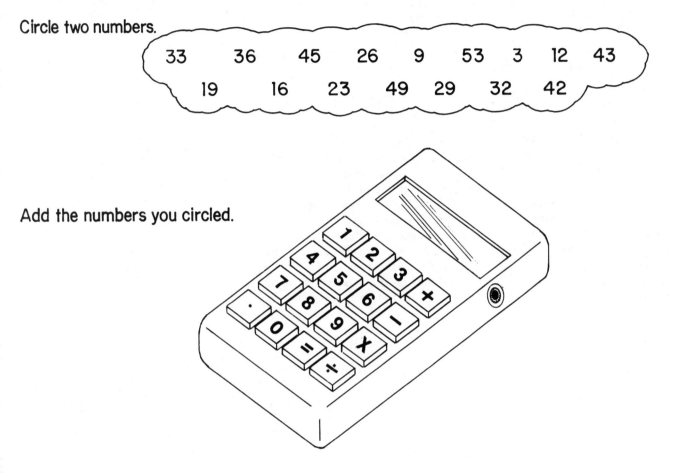

Find the box for your answer.

Keep track of your points.

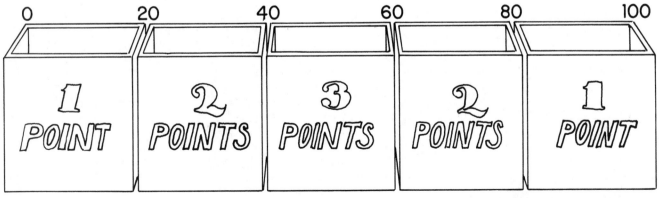

Levels: 1, 2, 3

Objective: Experience in estimating sums

Directons for teachers:

The way you use the activities will depend on the number of calculators available to you.

If you have one calculator:

1. Remove the master copy and reproduce a transparency for use with an overhead projector.

2. Project the transparency. Have students take turns selecting two numbers and using the calculator to find the answer.

3. Determine in which box the answer belongs and score the number of points listed on that box. The game is finished when all numbers have been selected once.

4. Play several games trying to improve the total class score each time.

If you have more than one calculator:

1. Remove the master copy and reproduce the worksheet.

2. Separate the students into teams with two teams sharing a calculator.

3. Have teams take turns selecting two numbers and using the calculator to find the answer.

4. Determine in which box the answer belongs and score the number of points listed on that box. The game is finished when all numbers have been selected once.

All the estimating activities may be modified for your students by changing the numbers at the top of each page or by changing the points for scoring the game at the bottom of each page.

After the students understand how to play the game, worksheets and a calculator could be placed in a learning center. The learning center provides the opportunity for students to work alone or in small teams to play the game.

Name _____

PLAY ESTIMATING MULTIPLICATION

Circle two numbers.

58	21	57	46	71	19	61	11
68	47	18	51	24	39	42	23
52	17	55	38				

Multiply the numbers you circled.

Find the box for your answer.

Keep track of your points.

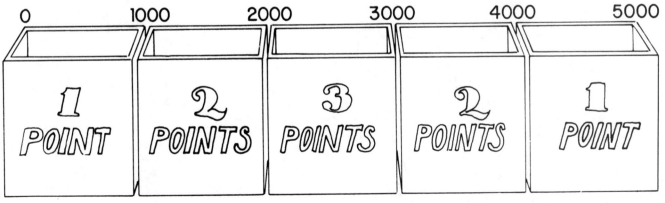

IDEAS For Teachers

Levels: 3, 4, 5
Objective: Experience in estimating products

Directons for teachers:

The way you use the activities will depend on the number of calculators available to you.

If you have one calculator.

1. Remove the master copy and reproduce a transparency for use with an overhead projector.

2. Project the transparency. Have students take turns selecting two numbers and using the calculator to find the answer.

3. Determine in which box the answer belongs and score the number of points listed on that box. The game is finished when all numbers have been selected once.

4. Play several games trying to improve the total class score each time.

If you have more than one calculator:

1. Remove the master copy and reproduce the worksheet.

2. Separate the students into teams with two teams sharing a calculator.

3. Have teams take turns selecting two numbers and using the calculator to find the answer.

4. Determine in which box the answer belongs and score the number of points listed on that box. The game is finished when all numbers have been selected once.

All the estimating activities may be modified for your students by changing the numbers at the top of each page or by changing the points for scoring the game at the bottom of each page.

After the students understand how to play the game, worksheets and a calculator could be placed in a learning center. The learning center provides the opportunity for students to work alone or in small teams to play the game.

Addition Game (2 teams)

How to play:

1. Teams take turns. Pick any two of these numbers

1	3	5	7	9	20
2	4	6	8	10	

2. Add the numbers you picked.

3. If the answer is on the game board, mark it with an X or O.

Game Board

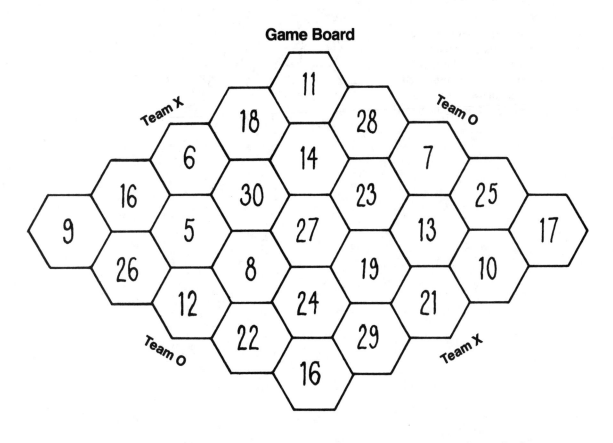

How to win: The first team to get a path across the game board wins.

Objective: Experience in addition

Levels: 1, 2

Directions for teachers:

The way you use the activities will depend on the number of calculators available to you.

If you have one calculator:

1. Remove the master copy and reproduce a transparency for use with an overhead projector.
2. Separate the students into two teams (team *X* and team *O*).
3. Project the transparency. Tell students there will be a five-minute warm-up before playing the game. During the warm-up session, students are to use their estimating skills to identify pairs of numbers whose answers (sums, differences, products, or quotients, depending on the game) are found on the game board.
4. To play the game, have the teams take turns selecting two numbers and using the calculator to compute the answer.
5. Each team finds its answer on the game board and puts the team's mark on it (*X* or *O*). The game is won when a team has an unbroken path of marked answers that connects its two sides of the game board (fig. 1).

If you have more than one calculator:

1. Remove the master copy and reproduce the worksheet.
2. Separate the students into teams, with two teams sharing a calculator.
3. Have teams take turns selecting two numbers and using the calculator to compute the answer.
4. Each team finds its answer on the game board and puts the team's mark on it (*X* or *O*). The game is won when a team has an unbroken path of marked answers that connects its two sides on the game board.

Comments:

Play the game more than once. At first students may pick pairs of numbers at random, but as they play more often they will start to develop strategies for using their estimation skills to select the numbers.

An interesting modification of the game is to require one player to pick the first number and another player on the same team to pick the second number.

Fig. 1

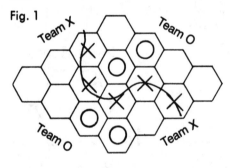

Add or Subtract Game (2 teams)

How to play:

1. Teams take turns. Pick any two of these numbers.

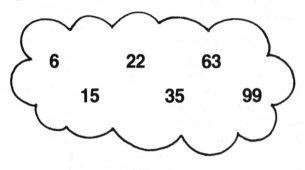

2. Add or subtract the numbers you picked.

3. If the answer is on the game board, place your team's mark on it (X or O).

Game Board

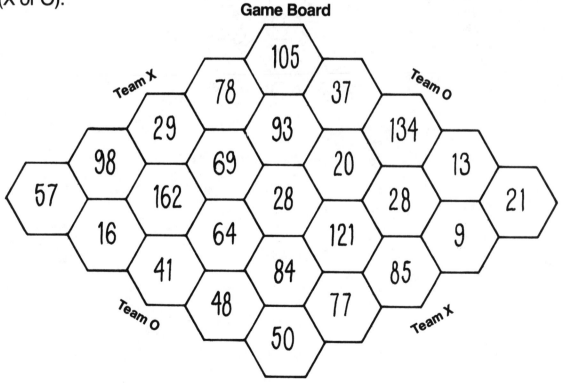

How to win: The first team to get a path of answers connecting its two sides of the game board wins.

 **For Teachers**

Objective: Experience in estimating sums and differences

Directions for teachers:

The way you use the activities will depend on the number of calculators available to you.

If you have one calculator:

1. Remove the master copy and reproduce a transparency for use with an overhead projector.

2. Separate the students into two teams (team *X* and team *O*).

3. Project the transparency. Tell students there will be a five-minute warm-up before playing the game. During the warm-up session, students are to use their estimating skills to identify pairs of numbers whose answers (sums, differences, products, or quotients, depending on the game) are found on the game board.

4. To play the game, have the teams take turns selecting two numbers and using the calculator to compute the answer.

5. Each team finds its answer on the game board and puts the team's mark on it (*X* or *O*). The game is won when a team has an unbroken path of marked answers that connects its two sides of the game board (fig. 1).

If you have more than one calculator:

1. Remove the master copy and reproduce the worksheet.

2. Separate the students into teams, with two teams sharing a calculator.

3. Have teams take turns selecting two numbers and using the calculator to compute the answer.

4. Each team finds its answer on the game board and puts the team's mark on it (*X* or *O*). The game is won when a team has an unbroken path of marked answers that connects its two sides on the game board.

Comments:

Play the game more than once. At first students may pick pairs of numbers at random, but as they play more often they will start to develop strategies for using their estimation skills to select the numbers.

An interesting modification of the game is to require one player to pick the first number and another player on the same team to pick the second number.

Fig. 1

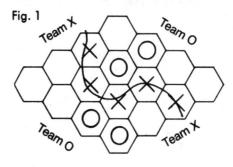

FIND THE VALUES

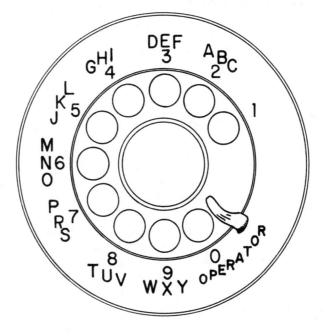

If you add the value of each letter (M = 6, A = 2, and so on), then MATHEMATICS is worth 52.

Find these:

APPLE = _____

NUMBER = _____

ADDITION = _____

SCHOOL = _____

RECESS = _____

SUNSHINE = _____

Write your first name below and find its value.

_____ = _____

"Find the Values"

Objective: To provide reinforcement in addition

Levels: 2, 3, 4, 5, 6

Answers: *number* = 32
           apple = 24
           addition = 36
           school = 30
           recess = 29
           sunshine = 45

Name _____

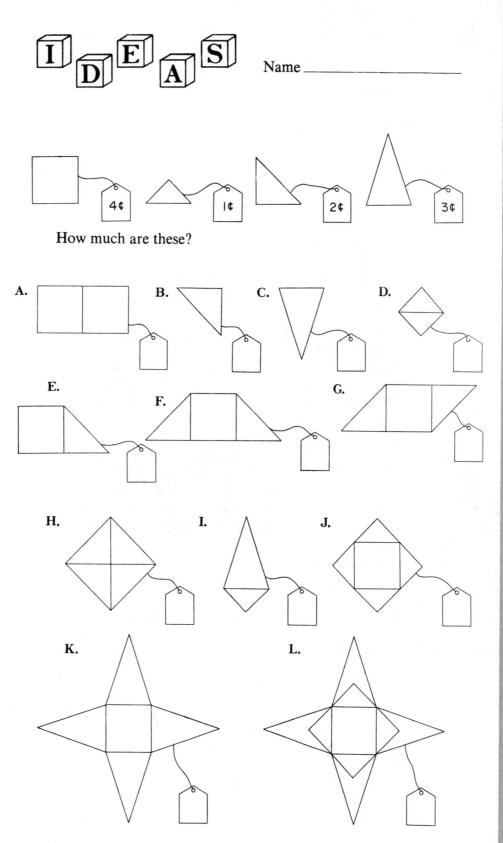

How much are these?

53

For Teachers

Objective: Experience with identification of congruent polygons

Grade level: 1, 2, 3, 4, 5, 6, 7, or 8

Directions for teachers:

Remove the student worksheet and reproduce a copy for each student.

For grades 1 and 2:

1. Discuss the square and triangles shown at the top of the page. Be sure to point out their cost.
2. Discuss the cost of the first four or five examples and fill in the tags.
3. Let the students do the rest of the examples on their own.

For grades 3, 4, 5, 6, 7, and 8

1. Have the students study the polygons at the top of the page and complete the price tags for the other polygons.
2. After they have completed the worksheet, discuss the relation between those polygons that are the same price. The area concept should come out in the discussion.

Comments: Fundamental to the development of many area concepts is the idea of conservation. In this case the area of a polygon does not change as we move it around or place it with other polygons. The use of price provides a different focus on area and forces the student to consider area in a different way. A variety of approaches to the development of a concept broadens the concept for some students and develops understanding for students that didn't see the idea before.

Answers

A. 8   B. 2   C. 3   D. 2   E. 6   F. 8   G. 8   H. 8   I. 4   J. 8   K. 16

Anticipate both 16 and 20 as answers for L.

Name _____

3¢   5¢   7¢

How much are these?

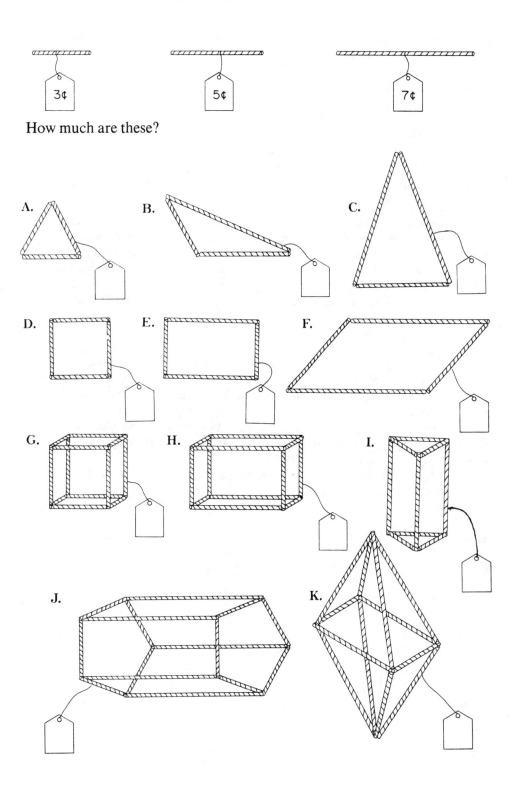

A.

B.

C.

D.

E.

F.

G.

H.

I.

J.

K.

Objective: Experiences with perimeter of polygons and identification of the edges of a solid

Grade level: 3, 4, 5, 6, 7, or 8

Directions for teachers:

1. Remove the student worksheet and reproduce one copy for each student.

2. After handing out the worksheet, ask the students to fill out the price tags on each figure.

3. When the students have completed their answers, discuss the different ways the students arrived at the answers: How did you know which straws make up the sides? Did you need to measure? Which polygons have the largest perimeters? What other polygons can you make from these straws? Can you make a polygon selling for 21 cents? For 13 cents? For 28 cents? What are possible prices for polygons made from these straws?

Comments: Students confuse the perimeter concept and the area concept because they don't have enough experience where the distinction is functional. There are few places in a student's life where he uses perimeter and area. An occasional contact in a classroom helps keep the distinction in mind. In many classes it would be appropriate to discuss the classification of triangles as equilateral, isosceles, or scalene. An investigation of pyramids, prisms, and other solids might also result.

Third and fourth graders would benefit by building some of the models, using straws and tape.

Answers

A. 9   B. 15   C. 19   D. 12   E. 16   F. 24   G. 36   H. 44   I. 33   J. 65   K. 72

Name _____

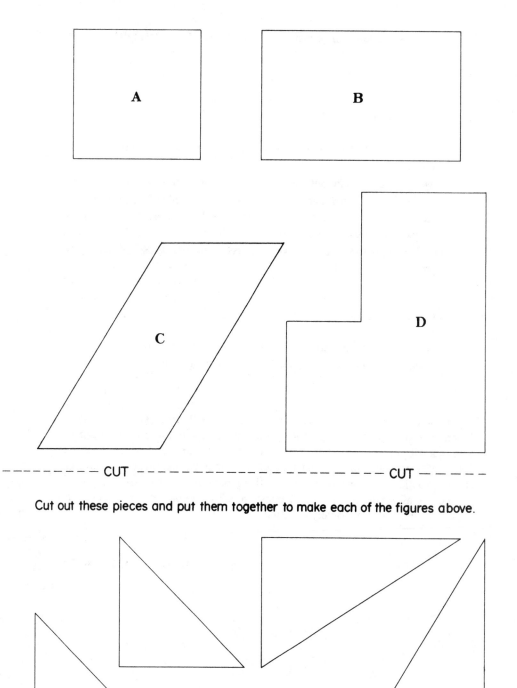

A

B

C

D

– – – – – – – – CUT – – – – – – – – – – – – – – – – – – CUT – – – – – –

Cut out these pieces and put them together to make each of the figures above.

Objective: Experience in constructing polygons out of triangles

Grade level: 1, 2, or 3

Directions for teachers:

1. Remove the student activity sheet and reproduce a copy for each student.
2. Have the student cut out the triangles at the bottom of his sheet.
3. Have the student form each of the polygons pictured. (The more mature students may work independently and draw line segments on the polygons to show how they constructed each.)
4. Use this opportunity to give special recognition to those students who are spatially oriented.

Directions for students:

1. Carefully cut out the triangles at the bottom of your activity sheet.
2. Use these triangles to make each of the polygons shown.

Comments: Several basic ideas are associated with this experience. Probably the most important in preparing the student for a study of area are the facts that all polygons can be formed from triangles and that most properties of triangles are unchanged even though the triangles are placed in different relative positions. Experiences such as these provide a very valuable change of pace for all students and a real boost in self-concept for the student who is spatially but not numerically oriented.

Cut out these pieces and make two squares.

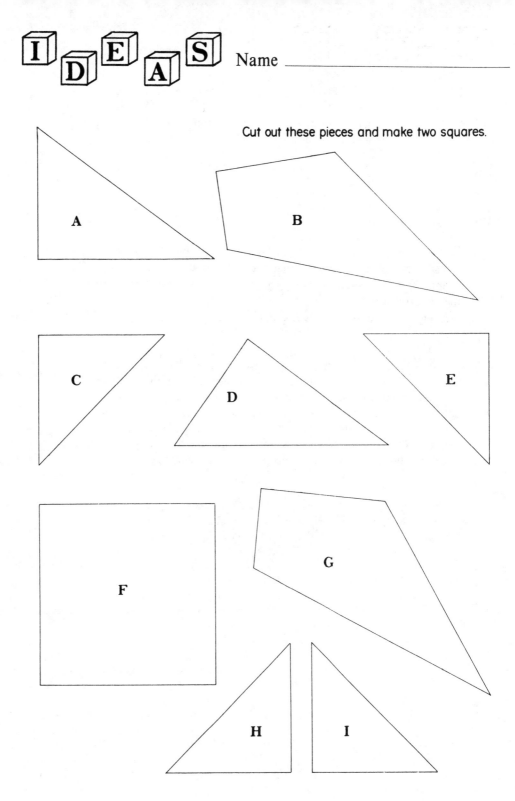

A   B   C   D   E   F   G   H   I

For Teachers

Objective: Experience in constructing a square from a variety of polygons,
              each containing at least one right angle

Levels: 3, 4, 5, 6

Directions for teachers:

1. Remove the activity sheet and reproduce a copy for each student.
2. Be sure students understand that they are to use all nine pieces in
   forming the two squares. (Polygon *F* is not one of the two squares
   they are to form!)
3. Encourage the students to work independently.

Comments: Though this activity could easily be viewed simply as a puzzle,
it is far more than that. The student who struggles with this activity has
personal experience with the basic concepts of congruence and tessellations.
The fact that the solution produces two squares that are the same size has
important though subtle implications for the sophisticated concept of area.
A skillful discussion leader may be successful in drawing out many generaliza-
tions from the students if he doesn't insist on precise language.

Solution

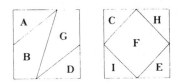

Name _____

Match a figure with each picture on the overhead projector.

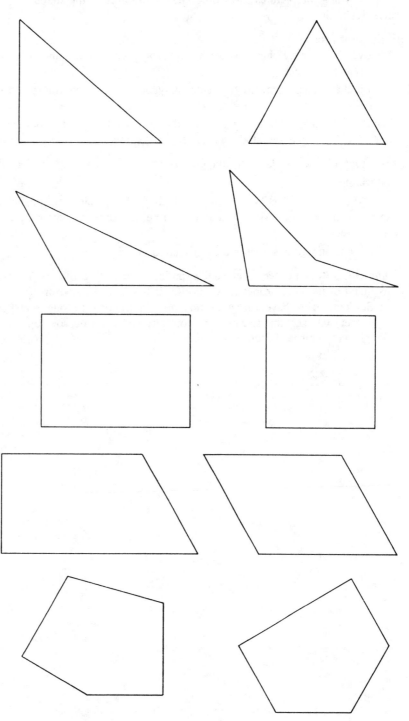

Objective: Experience in matching pictures of like shapes (similar polygons) when the pictures show different orientations of the shape.

Levels: 1, 2, or 3

Directions for teachers:

1. Remove the activity sheet. Make a copy for each student and a transparency for your use.

2. Cut up the transparency so that each polygon is on a separate piece of acetate.

3. Place the "transparent polygons" on the overhead projector one at a time. (Be sure that the student sees the image in a different orientation than that of the similar polygon on his paper: ◁   ▽ for the first triangle.)

4. Have the student identify the projected image by placing his finger on the polygon on his activity sheet that is "like" the one he sees projected on the screen.

5. Consider trying your students on the second activity sheet.

Comments: Students need personal experience in seeing that a polygon retains many of its basic properties even after it has been rotated or "flopped over." Students who have difficulty matching an image to one on their activity sheet will see the situation if you physically rotate, or flip over, the triangle on the piece of acetate.

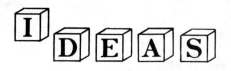

Name _____

Match a figure with each picture on the overhead projector.

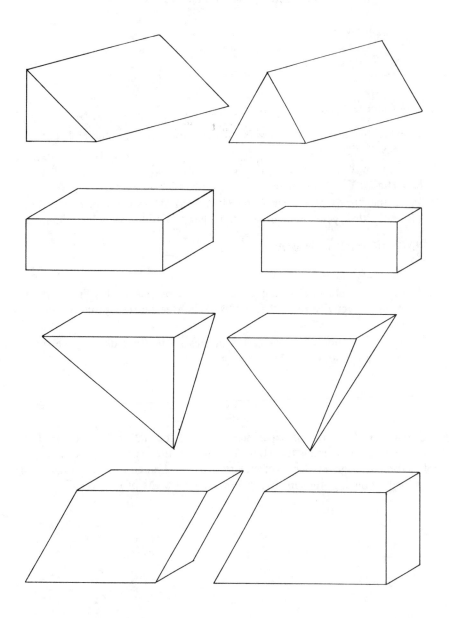

Objectives: Experience in matching pictures of a geometric solid when the pictures show different orientations of the solid.

Levels: 2, 3, or 4

Directions for teachers:

1. Remove the activity sheet. Make a copy for each student and a transparency for your use.
2. Cut up the transparency so that each polyhedron is on a separate piece of acetate.
3. Place the "transparent solids" on the overhead projector one at a time. (Be sure that your student sees the image in different orientation than

   that of the solid on his paper: or

   for the fourth solid.)
4. Have the student identify the projected solid by placing his finger on the solid on his activity sheet that is "like" the one he sees projected on the screen.
5. Be sure that some of the projected images result from flipping the transparency up-side-down on the projector.

Comments: This student experience in visual translations is not only fun, but excellent for helping the student focus on the basic properties of the polyhedra. Though student vocabulary will be limited, much insight can be gained by having students discuss how they view the projected solid.

Name _____

Connect points to make:

a square

a rectangle

a cross
(6 points)

5 points in a
straight line

a 5 point star

2 squares

 For Teachers

Objective: Experience in visualizing familiar geometric shapes

Levels: 1, 2, or 3

Directions for teachers:

1. Remove the activity sheet and reproduce a copy for each student.
2. Give each student a straightedge but don't require that he use it.
3. Read the instructions aloud. Be certain students understand that only some of the points are to be used for each drawing.

Comments: The focus of the activity is on *seeing* geometric shapes that have not been completely drawn. Be very receptive to the students' efforts. Don't be surprised if some of your nonnumerically oriented students show talent in activities involving spatial relations.

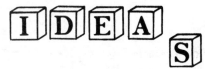

Use the points as corners:

- —draw a square
- —draw a rectangle
- —draw a triangle with equal sides.

Draw 3-point line segments:

- —that are parallel
- —that form a "T".
- —that form a triangle.

Objective: Experience in visualizing basic geometric objects

Levels: 3 or 4

Directions for teachers:

1. Remove the activity sheet and reproduce a copy for each student.
2. Be sure each student has a straightedge but do not require that he use it.
3. Be sure students understand that a 3-point segment is a line segment identified by the two endpoints and one point between.

Comments: Visualizing a rectangle or triangle with only the vertices (corner points) shown is a far more challenging experience than assigning a name to a picture. Some highly number-oriented students may experience frustration, while some of your nonnumerically oriented students may exhibit exceptional insight in spatial relations.

Key:

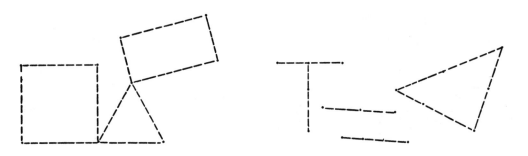

IDEAS

Name _____

COLORING SQUARES

You need crayons of two different colors. Color each 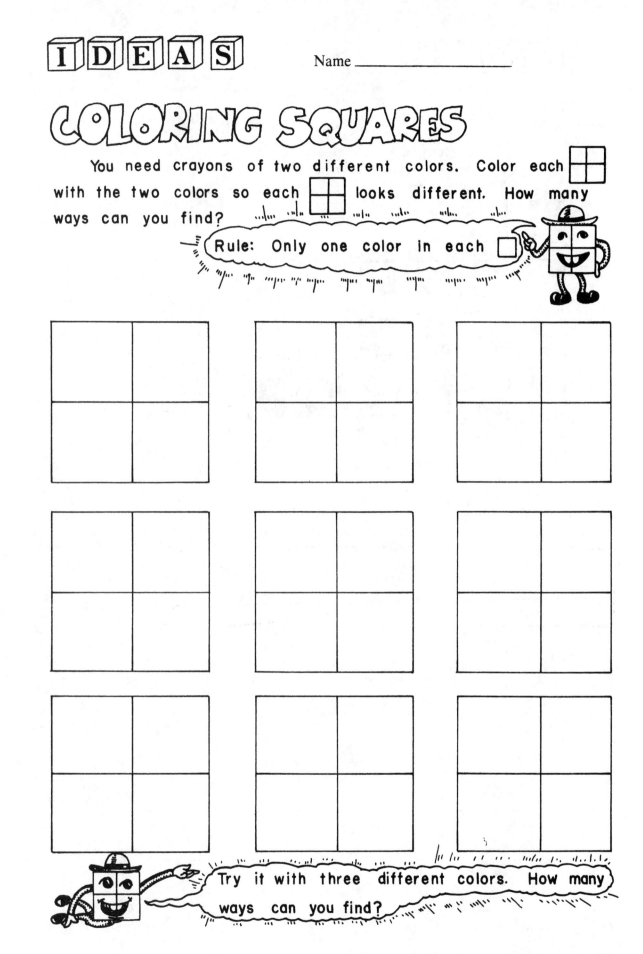 with the two colors so each looks different. How many ways can you find?

Rule: Only one color in each ☐

Try it with three different colors. How many ways can you find?

Coloring Squares

Levels 1, 2, 3

There are 16 ways to color a ⊞ with 2 colors.

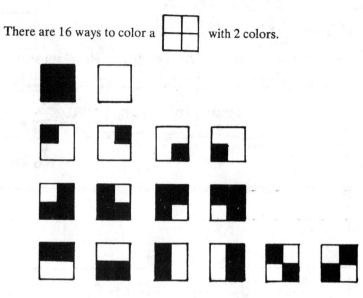

Name _____

In each row, choose two shaded regions that exactly cover the black region when you put them together.

Check your answers by cutting out the two shaded regions and laying them on top of the black region.

1.
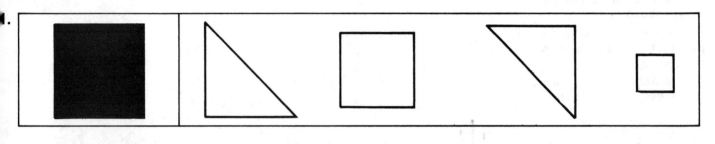

2.
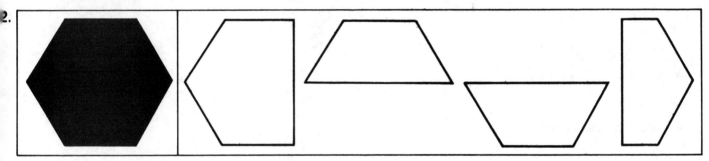

3.
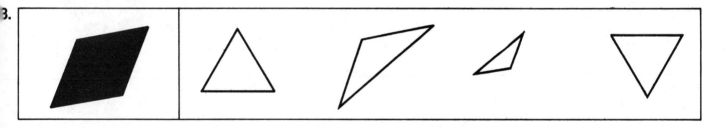

4.
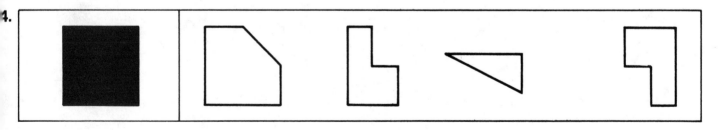

5.
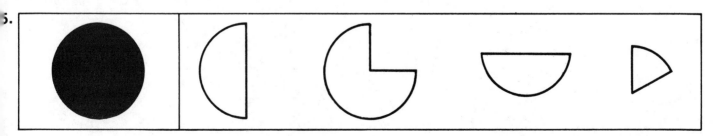

For Teachers

Objective: To practice covering regions to illustrate additivity of area.

Levels: 2, 3, 4

Directions for teachers:

1. Give each student a copy of the worksheet and scissors.

2. You may want the students to paste the two shaded regions on each black region.

3. In exercises 3 and 5, the shaded regions have to be rotated before they will fit.

Answers:

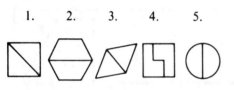

1.   2.   3.   4.   5.

Going further:

Ask students to make up puzzles like these.

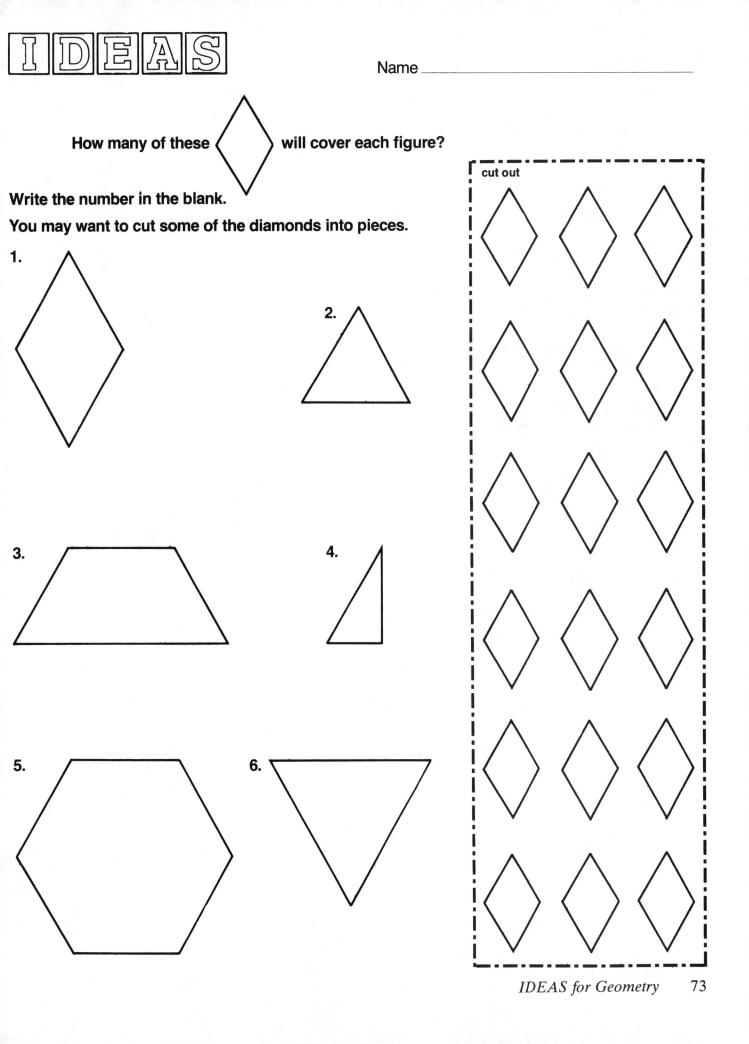

IDEAS

Name _____

How many of these ◇ will cover each figure?

Write the number in the blank.

You may want to cut some of the diamonds into pieces.

1.

2.

3.

4.

5.

6.

cut out

Objective: To measure areas by covering regions with a non-
standard unit.

Levels: 3, 4, 5

Directions for teachers:

1. Give each student a copy of the worksheet and scissors.

2. Be sure students understand that some of the diamonds may need to be cut into pieces in order to cover the figures completely.

3. Some students may prefer to work in small groups.

Answers: 1. 4 2. 2 3. 6 4. 1 5. 12
6. 4 1/2

Going further:

Ask students to make a figure that could be covered with 5 diamonds; 10 diamonds; or 20 diamonds.

How many blocks?

A._____

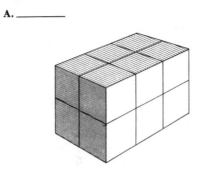

B._____

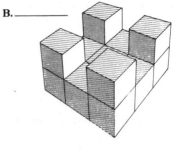

C._____

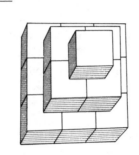

D._____

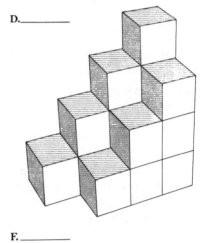

E._____

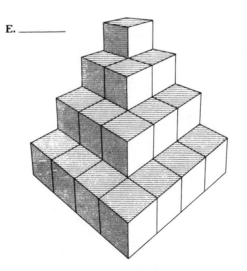

F._____

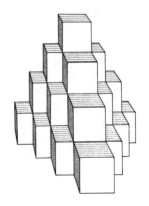

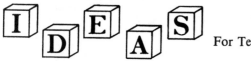 For Teachers

Objective: Experience in visualization of three dimensions

Grade level: 1, 2, or 3

Directions for teachers:

1. Remove the student worksheet and reproduce one copy for each student.
2. Provide one-inch cubes so that the student can check his visualization by construction.

Directions for students:

1. After studying each picture, decide how many blocks it would take to make the arrangement. Record your answer on your worksheet.
2. After you have finished all six examples, check your answers by making the arrangements with the cubes.

Comments: Since E requires 30 cubes you may want two or more students to work together in the second phase of the lesson. One-inch cubes are very useful visual aids in the primary class and can be used for many different activities. They are easily obtainable from most school supply houses and cost about four cents each in boxes of 100 cubes.

Name _____

Growing Up

Directions: Color the shapes as your teacher tells you to.

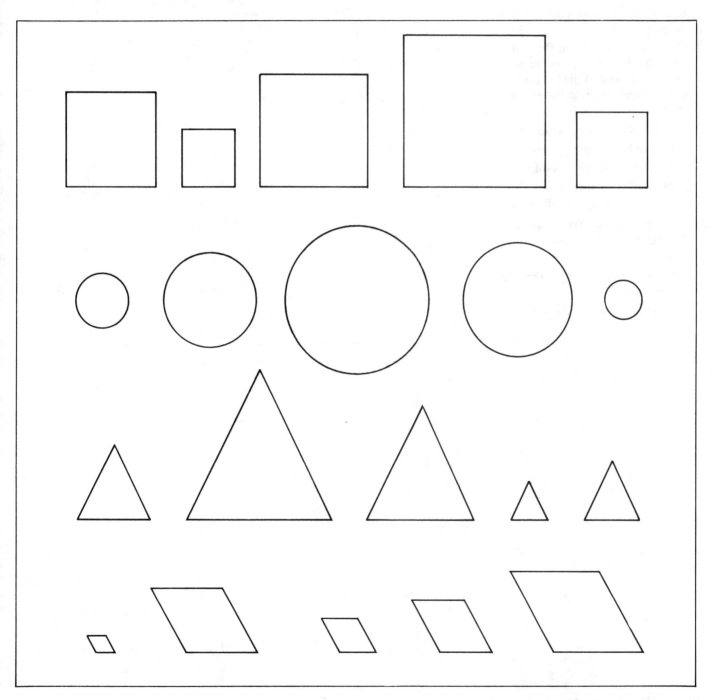

IDEAS For Teachers

Objectives: Classification of geometric shapes by certain measures.

Vocabulary development—*side, height, diagonal, diameter,* ....

Experience in using metric units to measure parts of the shapes.

Levels: 1, 2

Directions for teachers:

1. Reproduce the worksheet and give each child a copy.

2. Have the children color the shapes on each row by size, from the smallest to the largest. Write the colors in order where the children can see them:

smallest shape	blue
next smallest shape	green
next smallest shape	orange
next smallest shape	red
next smallest shape	yellow

3. As a check and for some possible discussion, you might ask the questions,

   What color is the largest shape in each row?

   What color is the middle-sized shape in each row?

Name _____

I D E A S

Put an X on the metric line for each of these measures.

Centimeters
0   10   20   30   40   50   60   70   80   90   100   110   120   130   140   150   160   170   180   190   200   210
Meters
0   1   2

10 centimeters   30 centimeters   35 centimeters   1 meter   1 meter   10 centimeters

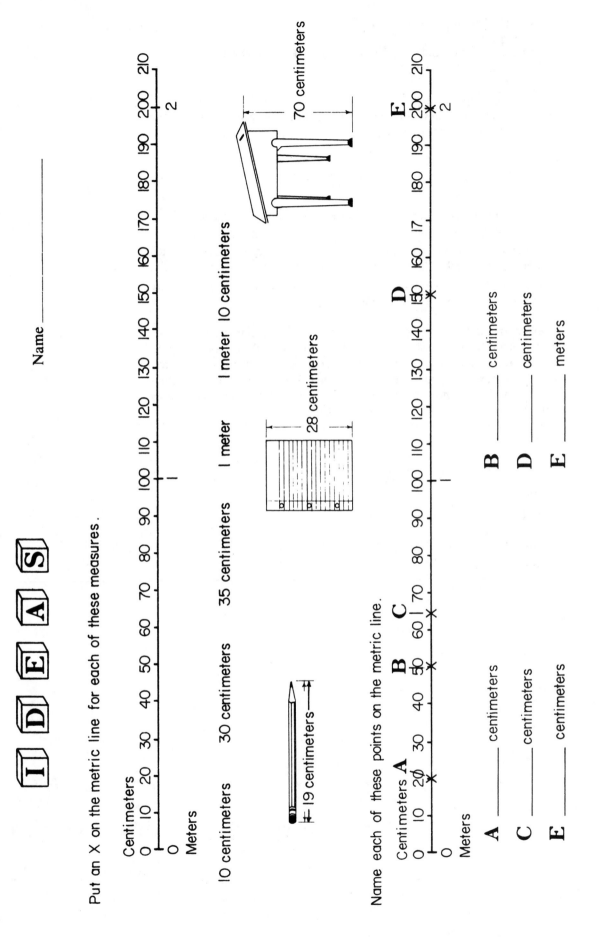

19 centimeters

28 centimeters

70 centimeters

Name each of these points on the metric line.

Centimeters   A   B   C
0   10   20   30   40   50   60   70   80   90   100   110   120   130   140   150   160   170   180   190   200   210
    X   X   X   X   X   X
Meters
0   1   2
                                                                                    D   E

A _____ centimeters   B _____ centimeters

C _____ centimeters   D _____ centimeters

E _____ centimeters   E _____ meters

 For Teachers

Objective: Experience in relating basic units of linear measure using a metric number line

Levels: 1, 2, or 3

Directions for teachers:

1. Remove the activity sheet. Reproduce a copy for each student.
2. Have a student measure with a meter stick the width or height of a familiar object in the front of the room. Have everyone put his pencil on his metric number line to show the measure reported by the student.
3. Be sure your students understand the directions for each part before they proceed.

Comments: Metric measures are likely to be more important to your students' lives than English measures. It is the school's responsibility to provide learning situations in which the student relates personally to metric units of measure. If your students have not had experiences in actual measurement with centimeter scales prior to this time, such experiences should precede the use of this activity sheet.

I D E A S

Name _____

Put an X on the line for each metric weight.

Grams
0   100 200 300 400 500 600 700 800 900 1000 1100 1200 1300 1400 1500 1600 1700 1800 1900 2000 2100

Kilograms
0 _____ 1 _____ 2

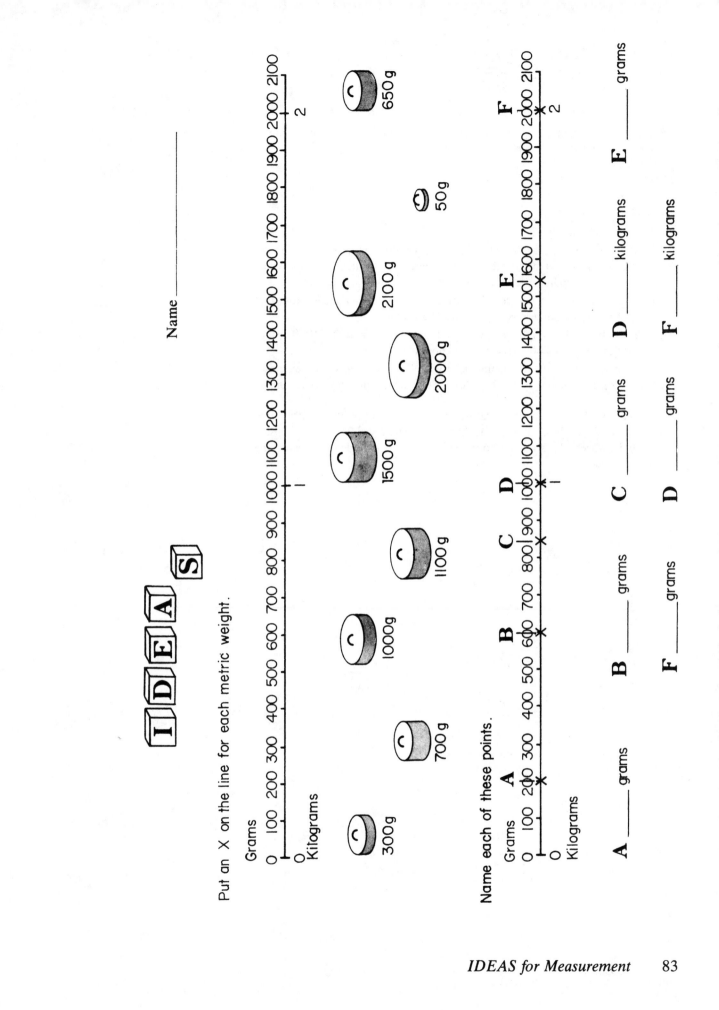

300g   700g   1000g   1100g   1500g   2000 g   2100 g   50g   650g

Name each of these points.

Grams
0   100 200 300 400 500 600 700 800 900 1000 1100 1200 1300 1400 1500 1600 1700 1800 1900 2000 2100
         A   B   C   D   E   F

Kilograms
0 _____ 1 _____ 2

A _____ grams   B _____ grams   C _____ grams   D _____ kilograms   E _____ kilograms

F _____ grams   D _____ grams   E _____ kilograms   F _____ kilograms

 For Teachers

Objectives: Experience in relating basic metric units of weight using a number line model

Levels: 2 or 3

Directions for teachers:

1. Remove the activity sheet and reproduce a copy for each student.
2. Hold up some familiar objects such as a chalkboard eraser labeled 52 grams and a book labeled 525 grams. Have each student use his pencil to show each weight on his metric number line.
3. Have students do the first set of exercises on the activity sheet. Note that the abbreviation for grams is used on the drawings.
4. Ask if any of the weights shown could have other names (1000 grams = 1 kilogram and 2000 grams = 2 kilograms).
5. Have students do the remaining exercises. The second set of exercises helps to focus on the two names for special points on the metric line.

Comments: These activities are not meant to replace experiences that build the student's basic referent for units of metric weight. Prior to using this activity sheet, the student should have personal experience in weighing familiar objects using metric scales.

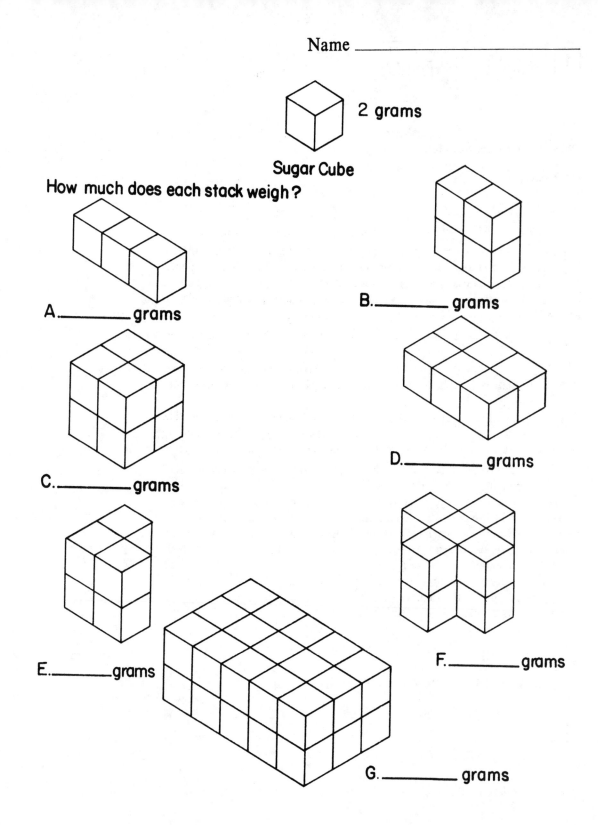

2 grams

Sugar Cube

How much does each stack weigh?

A. _____ grams

B. _____ grams

C. _____ grams

D. _____ grams

E. _____ grams

F. _____ grams

G. _____ grams

Objective: Experience with the metric system of weight

Grade level: 1, 2, or 3

Directions for teachers:

Remove the student activity sheet and reproduce a copy for each student. If feasible, each student should be given a sugar cube as a referent. Under less ideal circumstances, you may exhibit one or more sugar cubes to be sure that each student has at least a visual image of the object that weighs "2 grams."

Directions for students:

1. Note that each stack is made of sugar cubes and that each sugar cube weighs 2 grams.

2. Decide how much each stack weighs.

Comments: For sanitary and health reasons, it is impractical to have each student personally build and feel the weight of each stack of sugar cubes. This experience may easily be converted to a hands-on laboratory experience by using one-inch cubes that weigh approximately ten grams each. In classrooms where the students have had previous experiences with three-dimensional geometry, a work table with a box of wooden cubes will suffice as an aid for those students who can't visualize the stacks as pictured. Expect students to attack these problems in a variety of ways. Some will count by twos; others will find the number of cubes and multiply that number by two. Some students may solve *G* by simply multiplying the answer to *D* by five.

Answers

A. 6   *B.* 8   *C.* 16   *D.* 12   *E.* 12   *F.* 20   *G.* 60

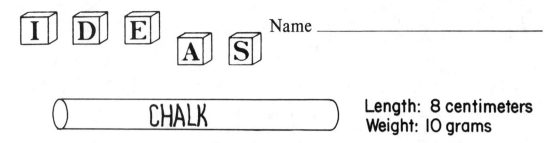
CHALK

Length: 8 centimeters
Weight: 10 grams

Estimate the total weight and the total length of the
pieces of chalk shown for each exercise.

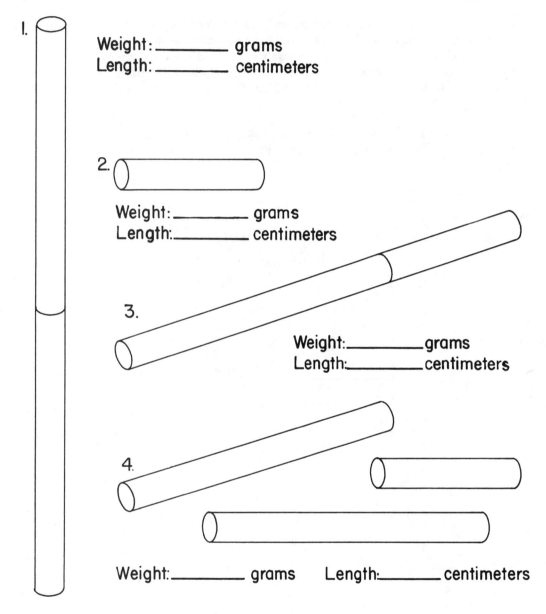

1.

Weight: _____ grams
Length: _____ centimeters

2.

Weight: _____ grams
Length: _____ centimeters

3.

Weight: _____ grams
Length: _____ centimeters

4.

Weight: _____ grams   Length: _____ centimeters

Objective: Experience with weight and length using the metric system

Grade level: 3 or 4

Directions for teachers:

Reproduce a copy of the activity sheet for each student. You may wish to exhibit or even pass around several new pieces of chalk. Students may note that most pieces of chalk are not identical and correctly conclude that the 8 centimeters and 10 grams are approximations. Once the students have the basic referent in mind they should work independently on this activity.

Comments: The total length as an end-to-end chain of individual pieces is an important concept. It should not be expected that this concept is intuitive for all students.

Answers

1. 20 grams, 16 centimeters   2. 5 grams, 4 centimeters
3. 15 grams, 12 centimeters   4. 25 grams, 20 centimeters

Name _____

BODY MEASURES

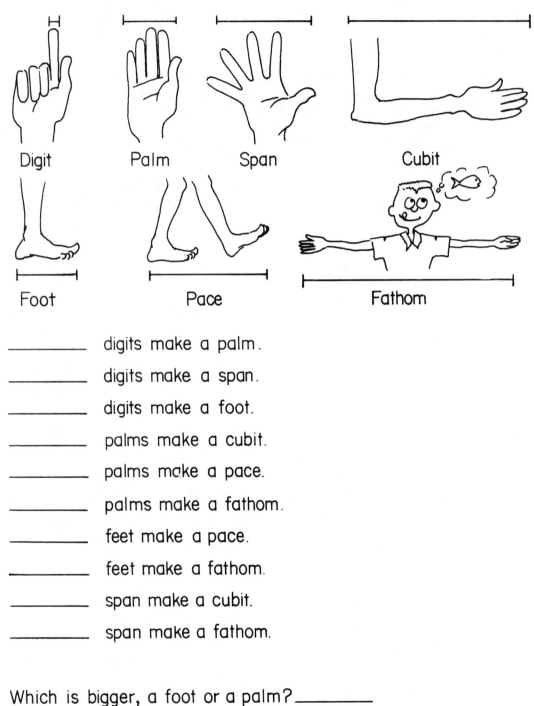

Digit   Palm   Span   Cubit

Foot   Pace   Fathom

_____ digits make a palm.

_____ digits make a span.

_____ digits make a foot.

_____ palms make a cubit.

_____ palms make a pace.

_____ palms make a fathom.

_____ feet make a pace.

_____ feet make a fathom.

_____ span make a cubit.

_____ span make a fathom.

Which is bigger, a foot or a palm? _____

Which is bigger, a foot or a span? _____

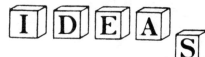 For Teachers

Objective: Experience in body measures and ratios.

Levels: 2 or 3

Directions for teachers:

1. Remove the activity sheet BODY MEASURES and reproduce one copy for each student.

2. Discuss the various body measures shown at the top.

3. Children are to compare their own measures and complete the sentences.

4. Discuss the completed findings so children can see how their measures are the same and different from those of others.

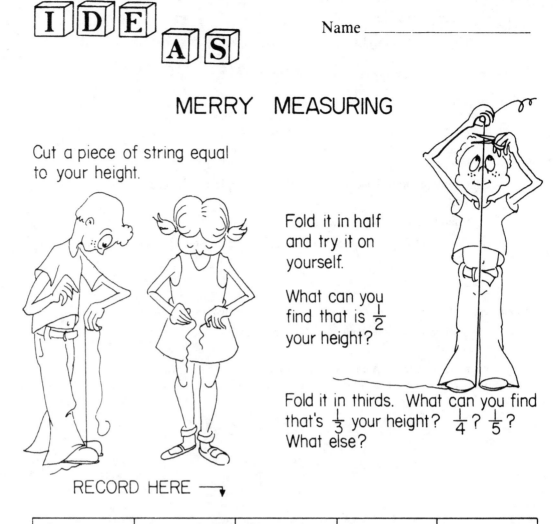

IDEAS

MERRY MEASURING

Cut a piece of string equal to your height.

Fold it in half and try it on yourself.

What can you find that is $\frac{1}{2}$ your height?

Fold it in thirds. What can you find that's $\frac{1}{3}$ your height? $\frac{1}{4}$? $\frac{1}{5}$? What else?

RECORD HERE ⟶

$\frac{1}{2}$ my height	$\frac{1}{3}$ my height	$\frac{1}{4}$ my height	$\frac{1}{5}$ my height	What else?

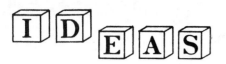

Objective: Experience with body measures and body ratios.

Levels: 3, 4, or 5

Directions for teachers:

1. Remove the activity sheet MERRY MEASURING and reproduce one copy for each student.

2. Discuss it to make sure the directions are understood.

3. Give each child a piece of string. Make sure the string doesn't have any stretch.

Follow-up:

Additional problems using the piece of string can be suggested.

(1) How many of your widest smile make your height? Guess first, then use your string.

(2) Did your mother ever wrap a sock around your fist to see if it was your size? Why would she do a thing like that? Use your string to see.

Name _____

ME AS A MEASURE

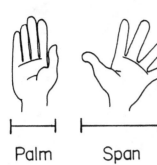
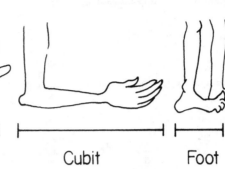
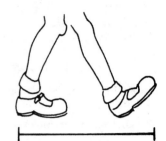

| Palm | Span | Cubit | Foot | Pace |

What to measure		Guess	Measurement
Door			
Desk Top			
Desk Height			
Chalkboard	square - - - - high - - - - -		
Book			

 For Teachers

Objective: Experience in estimating and doing body measuring.

Levels: 1 or 2

Directions for the teacher:

1. Remove the activity sheet ME AS A MEASURE and reproduce at least one copy for each student.

2. Discuss the various body measures at the top.

3. Children are to
   (1) choose *one* body measure and circle it; and
   (2) for each "What to measure," make a guess and then measure using the chosen body measure.

4. Children may repeat the activity using another body measure.

IDEAS for Problem Solving

IDEAS

Objective: Experience in writing and
solving "story" problems

Levels: 1–8

Directions for Teachers:

"The Zoo Keeper"

1. Distribute a copy of this sheet to
every student.

2. Have students read and fill in the
blanks on this sheet. (For younger
students, you may want to do this
activity together.)

My Problem-Solving Animal

M<small>Y STORY PROBLEM</small>: _____

_____

_____

_____

Author_____ Age____

Illustrator_____ Age____

School_____

I D E A S

Objective: Experience in writing and
                solving "story" problems

Levels: 1–8

Directions for Teachers:

"My Problem Solving Animal"

1. Distribute a copy of this sheet to
   every student.
2. Have students use the information
   they filled in on the "Zoo Keeper"
   to help them draw their animal and
   write a "story" problem about it.
3. Allow students to share their "Problem Solving Animal" problems
   with their classmates.

Name _____

NUMBER COLOR CLUES

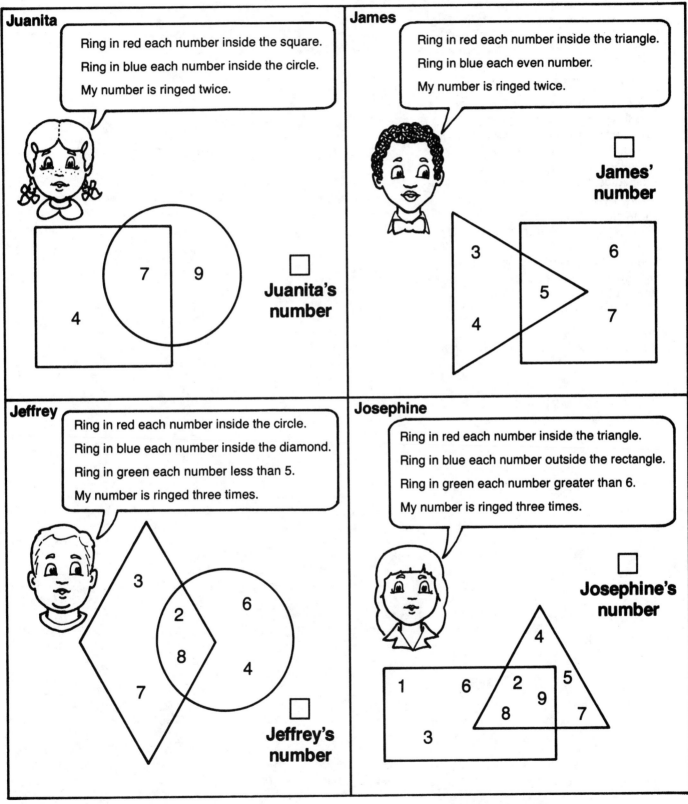

Juanita

Ring in red each number inside the square.

Ring in blue each number inside the circle.

My number is ringed twice.

☐ **Juanita's number**

7   9

4

James

Ring in red each number inside the triangle.

Ring in blue each even number.

My number is ringed twice.

☐ **James' number**

3   6

5

4   7

Jeffrey

Ring in red each number inside the circle.

Ring in blue each number inside the diamond.

Ring in green each number less than 5.

My number is ringed three times.

3

2   6

8   4

7

☐ **Jeffrey's number**

Josephine

Ring in red each number inside the triangle.

Ring in blue each number outside the rectangle.

Ring in green each number greater than 6.

My number is ringed three times.

☐ **Josephine's number**

4

1   6   2   5

9

8   7

3

Number Color Clues

Objective: To provide students an opportunity to use logical reasoning with the concepts of
inside, outside, even and
odd, less than, and greater
than.

Levels: 1, 2

Directions for teachers:

1. Give each student a copy of the
   worksheet, or make an overhead
   transparency and conduct the activity with the class as a whole.

2. You may want to read the directions
   to the students or pair good readers
   and poor readers.

3. The numbers that solve the puzzles
   will satisfy the two or three conditions simultaneously. Students will
   not have to be consciously aware of
   this, however, since the directions
   automatically account for this in a
   step-by-step fashion.

Answers:
Juanita, 7; James, 4; Jeffrey, 2; Josephine, 7

Going further:
Have students make up puzzles like
these for friends.

Name _____

TOP SECRET

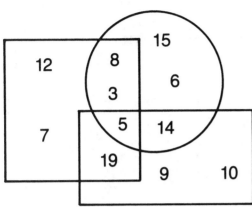

Each child has a secret number.
Can you find each number?

Harry

List the numbers inside the rectangle.

_____

List the numbers less than 8.

_____

My number is in both lists. ☐

Helen

List the numbers inside the circle.

_____

List the multiples of 7.

_____

My number is in both lists. ☐

Henrietta

List the numbers inside the square.

_____

List the numbers inside the circle.

_____

List the even numbers.

_____

My number is in all three lists. ☐

Herman

List the numbers inside the rectangle.

_____

List the numbers outside the square.

_____

List the odd numbers.

_____

My number is in all the lists. ☐

Horatio

List the numbers outside the circle.

_____

List the numbers outside the rectangle.

_____

List the multiples of 3.

_____

My number is in all three lists. ☐

Hortense

List the numbers greater than 9.

_____

List the odd numbers.

_____

List the numbers inside the rectangle.

_____

My number is in all three lists. ☐

Top Secret

Objective: To provide students an opportunity to use logical reasoning with the concepts of inside, outside, less than, greater than, and multiple of.

Levels: 3, 4

Directions for teachers:

1. Give each student a copy of the worksheet, or make an overhead transparency and conduct the activity with the class as a whole.

2. The secret numbers will satisfy the two or three conditions simultaneously. Be sure that students understand that the secret number for each puzzle must be in all the lists. In fact the secret number is the only number that is in each of the lists.

Answers:

Harry, 5; Helen, 14; Henrietta, 8; Herman, 9, Horatio, 12, Hortense, 19.

Going further:

Have students make up puzzles like these for friends.

I D E A S

Problem Solving Tic-Tac-Toe

Tic-Tac-Toe Board

Write my numbers in the Tic-Tac-Toe.

3
4   7   10
5   8   11
6   9

Pick any problem below.
Find the answer to the problem.
Put an *X* on the answer in the tic-tac-toe.
Three *X*s in a line wins.

Problems

You had 3 toy cars. Sue gave you 4 more. How many cars do you have?

You had 5 cents. You got 5 cents more. How many cents do you have?

You have 1 yellow pencil, 1 red pencil, and 1 blue pencil. How many pencils do you have?

There are 6 fish in a bowl.
There are 3 fish in another bowl.
How many fish altogether?

The park has 4 swings. It has 2 slides. How many things are there to play on?

Bill counted 5 boys playing kick ball. Ann counted 6 girls playing kick ball. How many are playing kick ball?

We had 2 bats. Coach has 6 new bats. How many bats do we have?

Your mom gave you 2 cookies. Your brother gave 1 more. Your sister gave you 1 more. How many cookies did you get?

You ate 2 hamburgers. Your dad ate 3 hamburgers. How many hamburgers were eaten?

IDEAS For Teachers

Objective: Experience in solving addition problems

Levels: 1, 2

Directions for teachers:

1. Remove the master and reproduce one copy for each student.

2. Students fill in their tic-tac-toe by randomly writing the numbers in the nine empty spaces.

3. Students choose any problem at the bottom of the page, solve it, and mark (X) the answer on their tac-tac-toe.

4. At the lower levels, students win with a simple tic-tac-toe (three Xs in a line vertically, horizontally, or diagonally). With older students, *two* tic-tac-toes (three Xs in a line twice) are needed to win.

Depending on your class, you may want to read the problems to your students. If the problems are read aloud, have the students select the order in which the problems are read.

The game may be played in partnerships. Players take turns selecting a problem, then mark their answer on the tic-tac-toe with either an X or O.

Problem Solving Tic-Tac-Toe

Tic-Tac-Toe Board

Fill in the spaces on the Tic-Tac-Toe with these nine numbers.

2 3 4 5 6 7 8 9 10

Now choose any problem below. Solve it.
Put an *X* on the answer on the tic-tac-toe board.
Three *X*s in a line wins.

Problems

Add 7 to my mystery number and you get 15. What's my mystery number?

Subtract 6 from my mystery number and you get 3. What's my mystery number?

Subtract 5 from my mystery number. Then add 8 and you get 10. What's my mystery number?

Add my mystery number to itself. Then subtract 4 and you get 0. What's my mystery number?

Subtract 7 from my mystery number and you get 3. What's my mystery number?

Add 17 to my mystery number and you get 20. What's my mystery number?

Subtract 3 from my mystery number. Then add 9 and you get 10. What's my mystery number?

Add 8 to my mystery number. Then subtract 8 and you get 5. What's my mystery number?

Add my mystery number to itself and you get 12. What's my mystery number?

 **For Teachers**

Objective: Experience in solving addition and subtraction problems

Levels: 3, 4

Directions for teachers:

1. Remove the master and reproduce one copy for each student.

2. Students fill in their tic-tac-toe by randomly writing the numbers in the nine empty spaces.

3. Students choose any problem at the bottom of the page, solve it, and mark (*X*) the answer on their tac-tac-toe.

4. At the lower levels, students win with a simple tic-tac-toe (three *X*s in a line vertically, horizontally, or diagonally). With older students, *two* tic-tac-toes (three *X*s in a line twice) are needed to win.

Depending on your class, you may want to read the problems to your students. If the problems are read aloud, have the students select the order in which the problems are read.

The game may be played in partnerships. Players take turns selecting a problem, then mark their answer on the tic-tac-toe with either an *X* or *O*.

Name _____

Cut along the dotted lines. Put each set of pictures in order.

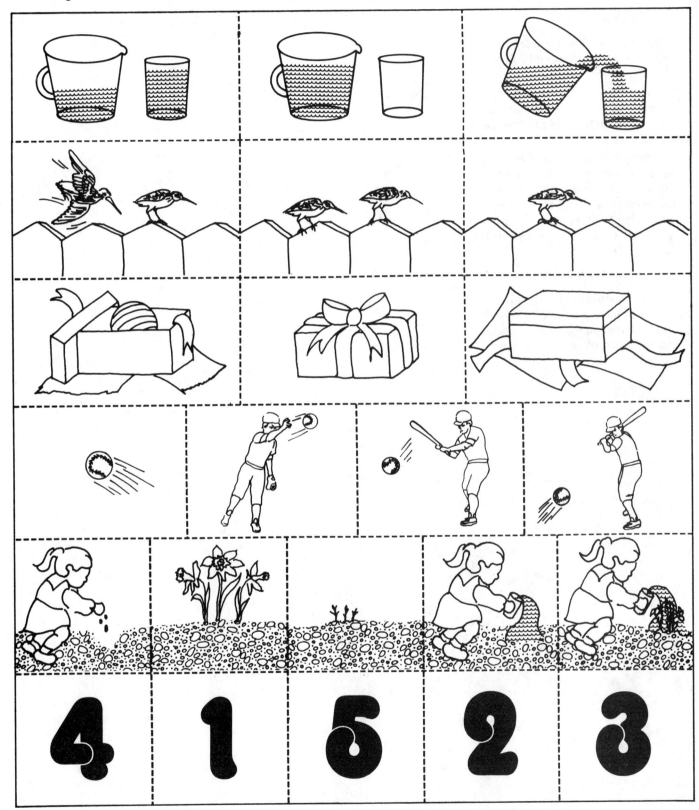

IDEAS For Teachers

Objective: To give students experience in ordering sets of pictures.

Levels: 1, 2

Directions for teachers:

1. Remove the master and reproduce one copy for each child. Provide scissors for students' use.

2. Go over the directions carefully; be sure students understand what to do and that each row of pictures is a separate set.

3. After each set of pictures has been put in order, discuss reasons for the set's order. For example, on the second row, first there was one bird on the fence; then another flew down; and then there were two birds on the fence.

Going further:

Provide construction paper and paste. Have students paste their sets of pictures in order on the paper. Display the mounted sets on the bulletin board.

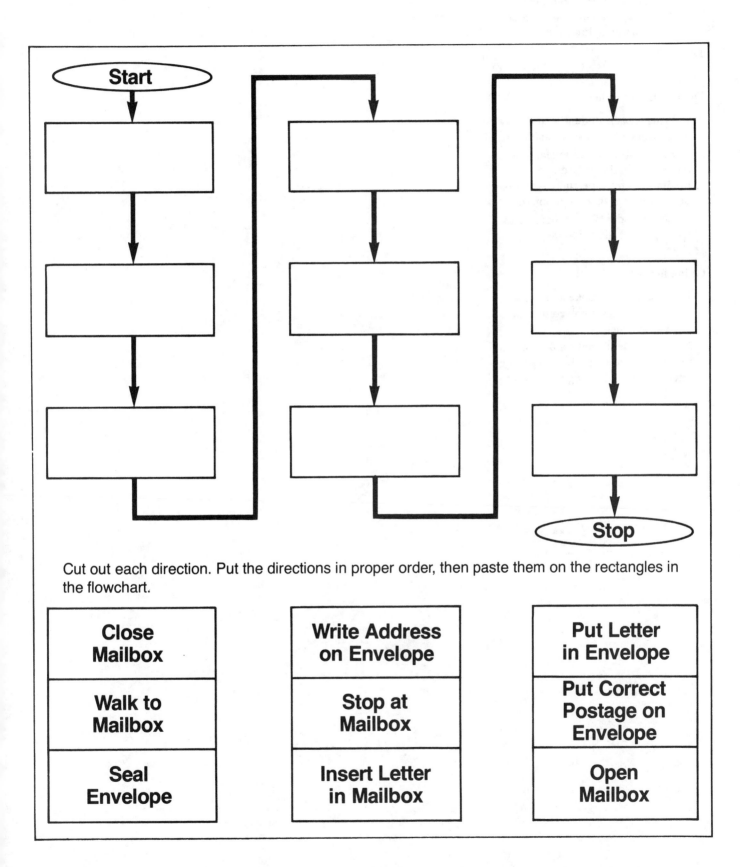

Cut out each direction. Put the directions in proper order, then paste them on the rectangles in the flowchart.

Close Mailbox	Write Address on Envelope	Put Letter in Envelope
Walk to Mailbox	Stop at Mailbox	Put Correct Postage on Envelope
Seal Envelope	Insert Letter in Mailbox	Open Mailbox

Objective: To provide students with experience in putting the steps of a procedure in order on a flowchart.

Levels: 3, 4

Directions for teachers:

1. Provide each student with a copy of the worksheet, scissors, and paste.

2. Be sure students understand the directions. In the procedure for mailing an envelope, there is an order to the steps that are followed.

3. Check students' work before the rectangles are affixed to the flowchart.

Going further:

1. Have students make a flowchart to show the steps involved in making a telephone call.

2. Have students make a flowchart to show the steps involved in getting out of bed and dressing in the morning.

Guess and Test

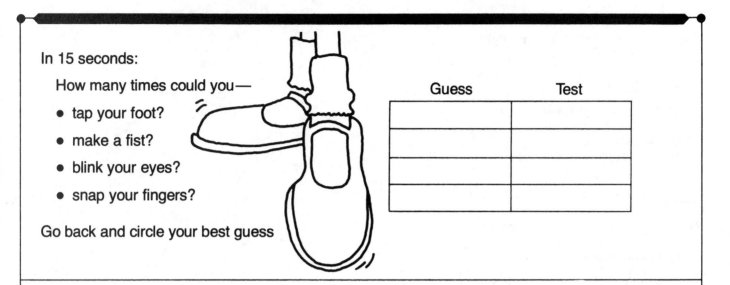

In 15 seconds:

How many times could you—

- tap your foot?
- make a fist?
- blink your eyes?
- snap your fingers?

Go back and circle your best guess

Guess	Test

In 30 seconds:

How far could you count by fives?

How many foods could you name?

How many times could you tie your shoe?

How many times could you tap your foot?

Go back and circle your best guess.

Guess	Test

In 60 seconds:

How far could you count by ones?

How many people in your class can you name?

How many numbers could your write?

How many times could you tap your foot?

Go back and circle your best guess.

Are you a good guesser? ☐ Yes ☐ No

Guess	Test

I D E A S

GUESS AND TEST

Objective

Experience in estimating quantities and gathering data.

Materials needed

• A clock or watch that measures seconds, or timers for measuring 15, 30, and 60 seconds
• One copy of the worksheet per student

Review

How to measure 15, 30, and 60 seconds

Directions for teachers

1. Ask each student to guess how many times he or she could do the activities in the 15-second category. Have them write their estimates in the "Guess" boxes.

2. Then have students work with partners to time one another in doing the activities.

3. Next students should compare their "Guess" and "Test" columns.

4. Have them follow the same procedure for the 30-second and 60-second questions.

5. When they have finished guessing and testing, ask them to circle their best guesses.

Extension

1. Have students make up Guess-and-Test activities of their own.

2. Make a class "Record Book" for these and other activities.

Name_____

Guesstimates

How long would it take you to—

- hop 10 times?

- snap your fingers 20 times?

- count backwards from 20?

- count by 5's to 100?

- write the numbers you say when you count by 2's to 50?

- tie your shoe 10 times? (or someone else's)

- write 40 X's on your paper?

- write your name, address, and telephone number?

	Guess	Test

Go back and circle your best guess.
Are you a good guesser? ☐ yes ☐ no

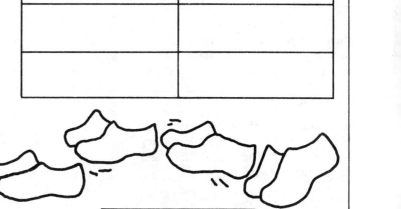

Would you believe—

Gary hopped 10 times in 5 seconds?

Ursula counted by 5's to 100 in 10 seconds?

Emily wrote by 2's up to 40 in 75 seconds?

Sheila counted backwards from 20 in 5 seconds?

Steve snapped his fingers 40 times in 3 seconds?

Yes	No

GUESSTIMATES

Objective

Practice in estimating quantities, gathering data, and inspecting data to find the most reasonable answer.

Materials needed

- A clock or watch that measures seconds
- Copies of the worksheet

Review

How to measure seconds and the number of seconds in a minute

Directions for teachers

1. Ask each student to guess how long it would take her or him to do each of the activities in the box at the top of the page. Have them write their estimates in the "Guess" column.

2. Have the students work with partners to time the activities.

3. For the second exercise, students should answer yes or no based on their past experiences. Have them discuss and defend each answer in this section.

Extension

Have students make up some exercises like those in the second section to try on each other. They should try them out on themselves first.

How many birthdays will your class have during the next year?

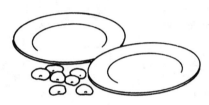

Draw 3 straight lines to cut the pie into 7 pieces.

How many ways can you put 7 lima beans on two plates?

There are 3 apples in the sack. How can you give one apple to each of 3 girls and yet leave one apple in the sack?

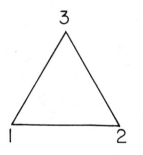

Place the numbers 1, 2, 3, 4, 5, and 6 on the sides of a triangle so all sides add to 9. (1, 2, and 3 are placed for you.)

Levels 1 or 2

Objective: Experiences in problem solving

Directions for teachers: (all levels)

1. Remove the activity sheet and make a copy of it.
2. Cut the problems apart and paste each one on a 5-by-7 card.
3. Suggestions for use:
   a. Post one as the "Problem of the Week." Post student solutions with next week's problem.
   b. Give one to each team of students. Have teams report their progress or solution.
   c. Give one to an individual as a special challenge or a special project.

Comments: Be receptive to partial solutions and incomplete reasoning patterns. Encourage students to test their ideas. Open-ended problems such as these often suggest other problems to the perceptive student. Encourage your students to create problems for your file.

Answer Key

—One birthday for each student (unless you have one on Feb. 29)

—

—Lima beans: 6 ways: (6, 1) (5, 2) . . . 8 ways if you include (7, 0) & (0, 7)
—Give the 3rd girl the apple in the sack

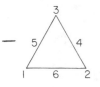

—

How many different ways can you have 25¢?

You have 10 points. How many line segments are needed to connect each pair?

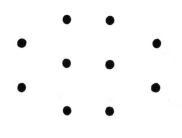

How many ways can you fold a piece of paper in half?

How many shapes can you make with 4 cubes?

Write 10 computational exercises that have the answer 144. Use +, −, x, and ÷, at least once in each exercise.

Levels 3 or 4

Objective: Experiences in problem solving

Directions for teachers: (all levels)

1. Remove the activity sheet and make a copy of it.
2. Cut the problems apart and paste each one on a 5-by-7 card.
3. Suggestions for use:
   a. Post one as the "Problem of the Week." Post student solutions with next week's problem.
   b. Give one to each team of students. Have teams report their progress or solution.
   c. Give one to an individual as a special challenge or a special project.

Comments: Be receptive to partial solutions and incomplete reasoning patterns. Encourage students to test their ideas. Open-ended problems such as these often suggest other problems to the perceptive student. Encourage your students to create problems for your file.

Answer Key

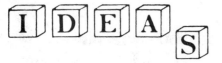

—25¢: 13 ways
—10 points: 45 line segments
—Endless number of ways. Any fold through point P.

![Square with point P and dashed fold lines through P]

—4 cubes: 8 shapes
—Examples: $100 \div 2 \times 3 + 10 - 16 = 144$; $75 \div 3 \times 8 - 70 + 14 = 144$